ALICIA WILL

Breaking Free from Relationship Doubts

*A Time and Experience Tested Path to Healing ROCD, and
building a solid future with your partner*

Contents

Introduction: Is It Me or Relationship OCD?

Love, relationships, and the journey of finding a life partner are central to the human experience. For many, these aspects of life bring joy, fulfillment, and a sense of belonging. However, for some individuals, what should be a source of happiness becomes a battleground of doubt, anxiety, and relentless questioning. If you've ever found yourself caught in a cycle of uncertainty about your relationship, constantly asking, "Is this the right person for me?" or "Do I really love them?", you might be experiencing more than just typical relationship jitters. You could be dealing with a condition known as Relationship Obsessive-Compulsive Disorder (ROCD).

This book aims to shed light on this often misunderstood and under-diagnosed form of OCD, helping you understand whether what you're experiencing is ROCD or simply the normal doubts that come with any relationship. By the end of this introduction, you'll have a clearer picture of what ROCD is, how it differs from regular relationship doubts, and the profound impact it can have on both your relationships and your self-esteem.

1.1 What is Relationship OCD?

Relationship OCD, often abbreviated as ROCD, is a subtype of Obsessive-Compulsive Disorder that centers around doubts and fears related to romantic relationships. While it's normal to have occasional doubts or concerns about a relationship, individuals with ROCD experience these thoughts in an intense, persistent, and distressing manner that significantly impacts their daily life and relationship satisfaction.

ROCD is characterized by two main components:

1. Obsessions: These are intrusive, unwanted thoughts, images, or urges that cause significant anxiety or distress. In the context of ROCD, these obsessions often revolve around:

- The "rightness" of the relationship
- The level of love or attraction felt towards a partner
- The partner's perceived flaws or shortcomings
- Comparisons with other potential partners or idealized relationships

1. Compulsions: These are repetitive behaviors or mental acts that a person feels driven to perform in response to an obsession. In ROCD, common compulsions include:

- Constantly seeking reassurance from a partner or others about the relationship
- Endlessly analyzing past interactions or feelings
- Comparing your relationship to others' relationships
- Repeatedly checking your own feelings or your partner's behaviors

It's crucial to understand that ROCD is not simply being indecisive about a relationship or having cold feet. It's a mental health condition that can cause significant distress and impairment in a person's life. People with ROCD often report feeling trapped in a cycle of doubt and anxiety, unable to fully engage in or enjoy their relationship despite genuinely caring for their partner.

ROCD can manifest in various ways. Some individuals may obsess over their own feelings, constantly questioning whether they truly love their partner or if they're attracted enough to them. Others may fixate on their partner's qualities, obsessing over perceived flaws or incompatibilities, no matter how minor. In some cases, ROCD can even affect single individuals, causing them to obsess over finding the "perfect" partner or avoiding relationships altogether due to fear of making the wrong choice.

It's important to note that ROCD can occur in any type of romantic relationship, regardless of gender, sexual orientation, or relationship duration. It can affect new relationships, long-term partnerships, and even marriages. The common thread is the persistent, intrusive nature of the doubts and the significant distress they cause.

1.2 How ROCD Differs from Regular Relationship Doubts

At this point, you might be wondering, "Don't all relationships involve some level of doubt or uncertainty?" You're absolutely right. It's entirely normal and even healthy to have occasional doubts or questions about your relationship. After all, committing to another person is a significant life decision, and it's natural to want to ensure you're making the right choice.

So, how can you tell if what you're experiencing is ROCD or just regular relationship doubts? Here are some key differences:

1. Intensity and Frequency:

- Regular doubts tend to come and go. They might arise during times of stress or conflict but generally subside when the situation improves.
- ROCD thoughts are intense, frequent, and persistent. They dominate your thinking, often occurring daily and lasting for extended periods.

1. Distress Level:

- Normal doubts might cause some unease, but they don't typically interfere with your daily functioning or overall happiness in the relationship.
- ROCD causes significant distress, anxiety, and often leads to depression. It can severely impact your ability to enjoy the relationship or even

function in daily life.

1. Focus of Concerns:

- Regular doubts usually focus on substantial issues that could genuinely affect relationship compatibility, such as differing values, life goals, or communication styles.
- ROCD often fixates on minor or irrelevant details. You might obsess over your partner's physical features, the tone of their voice, or try to quantify exactly how much you love them.

1. Reaction to Reassurance:

- When you have normal doubts, discussing them with your partner or friends often helps alleviate your concerns.
- With ROCD, reassurance provides only temporary relief. The doubts quickly return, often stronger than before, leading to a cycle of constant reassurance-seeking.

1. Impact on Decision-Making:

- Regular doubts might lead you to have productive conversations with your partner or make positive changes in your relationship.
- ROCD often leaves you feeling paralyzed, unable to fully commit to the relationship or to leave it, stuck in a limbo of constant questioning.

1. Presence of Compulsions:

- Normal relationship concerns don't typically involve compulsive behaviors.
- ROCD is characterized by compulsions like excessive checking of feelings, repeated comparisons with other couples, or constant seeking of external validation about the relationship.

1. Generalization:

• Regular doubts are usually specific to your current relationship and situation.
• Individuals with ROCD often find that their doubts and anxiety patterns repeat across multiple relationships or even when they're single.

1. Alignment with Values:

• Normal doubts generally align with your personal values and what you genuinely want in a relationship.
• ROCD thoughts often contradict what you truly value. You might logically know that your partner is a great match for you, but still be plagued by constant doubts.

Understanding these differences is crucial because the way you approach regular relationship doubts versus ROCD should be fundamentally different. Regular doubts can often be resolved through open communication, couples counseling, or personal reflection. ROCD, on the other hand, typically requires specialized treatment approaches, such as Cognitive-Behavioral Therapy (CBT) or Exposure and Response Prevention (ERP), which we'll discuss in later chapters.

1.3 The Impact of ROCD on Relationships and Self-Esteem

Relationship OCD can have profound and far-reaching effects on both your romantic relationships and your sense of self. Understanding these impacts is crucial for recognizing the seriousness of ROCD and motivating yourself or your loved ones to seek help.

Impact on Relationships:

1. Emotional Distance: ROCD can create an emotional barrier between partners. The individual with ROCD may withdraw emotionally as they

grapple with their doubts, leaving their partner feeling confused and rejected.

2. Communication Breakdown: The constant need for reassurance and the difficulty in expressing ROCD thoughts can strain communication. Partners may feel overwhelmed or frustrated by the repetitive nature of ROCD-related discussions.

3. Loss of Intimacy: Both emotional and physical intimacy can suffer. The person with ROCD might avoid physical closeness due to their doubts, while their partner may feel unloved or unattractive.

4. Trust Issues: The constant questioning inherent in ROCD can erode trust in the relationship. The non-ROCD partner may start to doubt the stability of the relationship or their partner's feelings for them.

5. Relationship Instability: ROCD can lead to a pattern of breaking up and getting back together as the individual oscillates between doubts and moments of clarity.

6. Avoidance of Commitment: For those not yet in committed relationships, ROCD can lead to avoiding long-term commitments altogether, missing out on potentially fulfilling partnerships.

Impact on Self-Esteem:

1. Self-Doubt: Constantly questioning your feelings and decisions can lead to a pervasive sense of self-doubt that extends beyond your relationship.

2. Guilt and Shame: Many individuals with ROCD feel intense guilt about their thoughts, especially if they believe they should be feeling differently about their partner.

3. Lowered Self-Worth: The inability to "control" your thoughts or "just be happy" in your relationship can lead to feelings of inadequacy and lowered self-esteem.

4. Anxiety and Depression: The constant state of uncertainty and the exhausting nature of ROCD thoughts can contribute to the development or exacerbation of anxiety and depression.

5. Identity Confusion: ROCD can make you question not just your

relationship, but your own identity, values, and desires, leading to a sense of disconnection from yourself.

6. Social Isolation: The all-consuming nature of ROCD thoughts can lead to withdrawal from friends and family, further impacting self-esteem and support systems.
7. Career and Personal Goal Disruption: The mental energy consumed by ROCD can interfere with work performance and the pursuit of personal goals, potentially affecting your sense of accomplishment and self-worth.

Understanding the serious impact of ROCD is the first step towards seeking help and reclaiming your life and relationships. It's crucial to remember that ROCD is a mental health condition, not a character flaw or a sign of not loving your partner enough. With proper treatment and support, it's possible to manage ROCD symptoms, improve your relationships, and rebuild your self-esteem.

In the following chapters, we'll delve deeper into the nature of ROCD, explore its causes and manifestations, and most importantly, discuss effective strategies for managing and overcoming this challenging condition. Whether you're dealing with ROCD yourself, supporting a loved one, or simply seeking to understand this condition better, this book will provide you with the knowledge and tools to navigate the complex landscape of Relationship OCD.

Remember, questioning "Is it me or ROCD?" is the first step on your journey towards clarity, healthier relationships, and a stronger sense of self. Let's embark on this journey together.

Understanding Obsessive-Compulsive Disorder (OCD)

To fully grasp the nature of Relationship OCD (ROCD), it's crucial to first understand its parent condition: Obsessive-Compulsive Disorder (OCD). This chapter will explore the fundamentals of OCD, its various types, and how ROCD fits into this broader spectrum of disorders.

2.1 The Basics of OCD

Obsessive-Compulsive Disorder is a mental health condition characterized by persistent, intrusive thoughts (obsessions) and repetitive behaviors or mental acts (compulsions) that an individual feels compelled to perform in response to these thoughts. While it's normal for people to occasionally have intrusive thoughts or engage in repetitive behaviors, individuals with OCD experience these symptoms to such an extent that they significantly interfere with daily life.

Obsessions

Obsessions are unwanted, intrusive thoughts, images, or urges that cause significant anxiety or distress. These thoughts are not simply excessive worries about real-life problems. Instead, they are persistent and often irrational ideas that intrude into a person's consciousness. Common themes of obsessions include:

1. Contamination: Fear of germs, dirt, or environmental contaminants
2. Harm: Fear of harming oneself or others, either accidentally or intentionally
3. Symmetry and order: Need for things to be arranged in a specific way
4. Forbidden or taboo thoughts: Intrusive thoughts about sex, religion, or violence
5. Doubting and uncertainty: Constant questioning of one's actions or decisions

It's important to note that having intrusive thoughts doesn't mean a person wants to act on them. In fact, individuals with OCD are often deeply disturbed by these thoughts and recognize them as irrational.

Compulsions

Compulsions are repetitive behaviors or mental acts that a person feels driven to perform in response to an obsession or according to rigid rules. These actions are aimed at preventing or reducing anxiety or distress, or preventing some dreaded event or situation. However, these compulsions are excessive and not realistically connected to the fears they're intended to address. Common compulsions include:

1. Cleaning and washing: Excessive hand washing, showering, or cleaning of objects
2. Checking: Repeatedly checking locks, appliances, or one's own body for signs of illness
3. Counting or repeating: Needing to perform actions a certain number of times

4. Ordering and arranging: Needing objects to be in a specific order or symmetry

5. Seeking reassurance: Repeatedly asking for confirmation that every-thing is okay

The OCD Cycle

OCD operates in a cycle that perpetuates itself:

1. Trigger: An event, thought, or situation that sparks an obsessive thought
2. Obsession: The intrusive thought causes anxiety or distress
3. Anxiety: The individual experiences increasing anxiety or discomfort
4. Compulsion: To alleviate the anxiety, the person performs a compulsive act
5. Temporary relief: The compulsion provides short-term relief from anxiety
6. Reinforcement: The cycle is strengthened, making it more likely to repeat

Understanding this cycle is crucial for both individuals with OCD and their loved ones, as it forms the basis for many treatment approaches.

Diagnosis and Prevalence

OCD is diagnosed when obsessions and compulsions:
- Take up significant time (more than an hour a day)
- Cause significant distress
- Interfere with daily life, work, or relationships

According to the National Institute of Mental Health, OCD affects about

1.2% of adults in the United States in any given year. It typically begins in childhood, adolescence, or early adulthood, with the average age of onset being 19 years old.

2.2 Types of OCD

While OCD can manifest in countless ways, researchers and clinicians have identified several common subtypes. It's important to note that many individuals with OCD experience symptoms from multiple subtypes. Here are some of the most recognized types of OCD:

1. Contamination OCD:
   This subtype involves fears of contamination and compulsive cleaning. Individuals may fear germs, bodily fluids, chemicals, or other substances they believe could cause illness or harm.

2. Checking OCD:
   People with this subtype feel compelled to check things repeatedly to prevent harm or disasters. This could involve checking locks, appliances, or even their own memories to ensure nothing bad has happened.

3. Symmetry and Ordering OCD:
   This involves a need for things to be arranged in a particular way. People may feel extreme discomfort if objects aren't lined up correctly or if things aren't in the "right" place.

4. Harm OCD:
   Individuals with this subtype experience intrusive thoughts about harming themselves or others. They may avoid situations or objects they fear could lead to harm, despite having no actual desire to hurt anyone.

5. Pure O:
   "Pure O" refers to OCD that is primarily obsessional, with mental rituals

rather than observable compulsions. However, mental compulsions are still present, such as mental reviewing or counting.

6. Scrupulosity:

This subtype involves obsessions related to religion, morality, and ethics. Individuals may fear that they've committed blasphemy or violated their moral code in some way.

7. Somatic OCD:

This involves obsessive fears about one's body and health. People may constantly monitor their bodily sensations and fear that normal physical experiences are signs of a serious illness.

8. Hoarding:

While now classified as a separate disorder in the DSM-5, hoarding was traditionally considered a subtype of OCD. It involves difficulty discarding possessions and excessive acquisition of items.

9. Relationship OCD (ROCD):

This subtype, which is the focus of this book, involves persistent doubts about one's relationship or partner.

Understanding these subtypes can help individuals recognize their symptoms and seek appropriate treatment. It's also worth noting that many people experience symptoms from multiple subtypes, and symptoms can change over time.

2.3 How ROCD Fits into the OCD Spectrum

Relationship OCD (ROCD) is a subtype of OCD that has gained increasing recognition in recent years. It fits into the OCD spectrum by following the same basic pattern of obsessions and compulsions, but with a specific focus on romantic relationships.

Obsessions in ROCD

In ROCD, obsessions typically revolve around:
  - The "rightness" of the relationship
  - The level of love or attraction felt towards a partner
  - The partner's perceived flaws or shortcomings
  - Comparisons with other potential partners or idealized relationships

These obsessions follow the same pattern as other OCD subtypes: they are intrusive, unwanted, and cause significant distress.

Compulsions in ROCD

Compulsions in ROCD often take the form of:
  - Repeatedly seeking reassurance from a partner or others about the relationship
  - Excessively analyzing past interactions or feelings
  - Comparing your relationship to others' relationships
  - Repeatedly "checking" your own feelings or your partner's behaviors

Like other OCD compulsions, these behaviors are aimed at reducing anxiety but ultimately reinforce the obsessive-compulsive cycle.

ROCD and Other OCD Subtypes

ROCD often coexists with or shares features with other OCD subtypes:

1. Checking OCD: ROCD can involve "checking" behaviors, such as repeatedly asking a partner if they love you or mentally reviewing past interactions for signs of problems.

2. Pure O: Many ROCD compulsions are mental rather than physical, similar to Pure O OCD. For example, mentally comparing your partner to others or

analyzing your feelings.

3. Harm OCD: Some individuals with ROCD fear that they might hurt their partner emotionally by not loving them enough or by leaving them.

4. Contamination OCD: In some cases, ROCD can involve fears of emotional or relational "contamination," such as worrying that exposure to attractive people might taint one's feelings for their partner.

ROCD in the Context of OCD Treatment

Understanding ROCD as part of the OCD spectrum is crucial for effective treatment. Many of the evidence-based treatments used for other forms of OCD, such as Exposure and Response Prevention (ERP) and Cognitive-Behavioral Therapy (CBT), are also effective for ROCD when tailored to relationship-specific obsessions and compulsions.

The Importance of Recognizing ROCD

Recognizing ROCD as a legitimate subtype of OCD is important for several reasons:

1. Validation: It helps individuals understand that their experiences are part of a recognized condition, not a personal failing.

2. Appropriate Treatment: Understanding ROCD as a form of OCD guides individuals towards effective, OCD-specific treatments rather than general relationship counseling, which may not address the underlying OCD mechanisms.

3. Differential Diagnosis: Recognizing ROCD helps distinguish it from other relationship issues or mental health conditions, leading to more accurate diagnosis and treatment.

4. Research and Understanding: Acknowledging ROCD as part of the OCD spectrum encourages further research and understanding of this specific manifestation of OCD.

In conclusion, while ROCD focuses on a specific content area (relationships), it follows the same fundamental patterns as other forms of OCD. It involves intrusive, distressing thoughts (obsessions) and behaviors aimed at reducing anxiety (compulsions), which ultimately reinforce the cycle. By understanding ROCD in the context of the broader OCD spectrum, individuals can better understand their experiences and seek appropriate, effective treatment.

As we delve deeper into the specifics of ROCD in the following chapters, keep in mind this broader context of OCD. Understanding the underlying mechanisms of OCD will provide a solid foundation for exploring the unique challenges and treatment approaches for Relationship OCD.

Signs and Symptoms of Relationship OCD

Relationship OCD (ROCD) can be a perplexing and distressing condition, often misunderstood as simply being "unsure" about a relationship. However, the signs and symptoms of ROCD go far beyond normal relationship doubts. In this chapter, we'll explore the common obsessions and compulsions associated with ROCD, and we'll look at real-life examples to help you better understand how this condition manifests in everyday life.

3.1 Common Obsessions in ROCD

Obsessions in ROCD are intrusive, unwanted thoughts, images, or urges that cause significant anxiety or distress. These obsessions often center around doubts about the relationship or the partner. Here are some of the most common obsessions experienced by individuals with ROCD:

1. Doubts about love:

- "Do I really love my partner?"
- "Am I in love enough?"
- "What if I'm mistaking comfort for love?"

1. Concerns about partner's feelings:

- "Does my partner truly love me?"

- "What if they're just settling for me?"
- "Are they as committed to this relationship as I am?"

1. Questioning relationship rightness:

- "Is this the right relationship for me?"
- "What if I'm making a huge mistake by staying?"
- "Should I be with someone else?"

1. Fixation on partner's flaws:

- Obsessing over physical imperfections
- Constantly noticing and ruminating on personality quirks
- Questioning whether you can accept these flaws long-term

1. Comparisons with other relationships:

- "Are other couples happier than we are?"
- "Would I be better off with someone else?"
- Constantly comparing your relationship to idealized notions of love

1. Doubts about sexual attraction:

- "Am I attracted enough to my partner?"
- "What if I find someone else more attractive?"
- Constant questioning of your level of sexual desire

1. Fears about compatibility:

- "Are we truly compatible?"
- "What if our differences are too significant?"
- Obsessing over small disagreements or differing interests

1. Concerns about relationship history:

- "What if I never get over my ex?"
- "Am I still in love with someone from my past?"
- Constantly comparing current relationship to past ones

1. Worries about future:

- "Will we be happy together in the long run?"
- "What if we grow apart?"
- Obsessing over potential future problems

1. Fears of hurting partner:

- "What if I'm leading them on?"
- "Am I a bad person for having these doubts?"
- Worrying about causing emotional pain to your partner

It's important to note that while many people experience some of these thoughts occasionally, individuals with ROCD find these obsessions to be frequent, intense, and highly distressing. The thoughts feel uncontrollable and significantly interfere with their ability to enjoy the relationship.

3.2 Common Compulsions in ROCD

Compulsions in ROCD are repetitive behaviors or mental acts that a person feels driven to perform in response to their obsessions. These compulsions are aimed at reducing anxiety or preventing some dreaded event, but they ultimately reinforce the obsessive-compulsive cycle. Here are some common compulsions seen in ROCD:

1. Seeking reassurance:

- Repeatedly asking your partner if they love you
- Constantly seeking validation about the relationship from friends or family
- Asking others about their relationships for comparison

1. Excessive analyzing:

- Replaying conversations or interactions in your mind to look for "signs"
- Analyzing your feelings constantly to check if you're "in love enough"
- Overthinking every aspect of the relationship

1. Comparison behaviors:

- Constantly comparing your relationship to others' relationships
- Comparing your partner to other potential partners or exes
- Searching for "perfect" relationships in media or real life to measure against

1. Testing behaviors:

- Intentionally thinking about other people to see if you feel attracted to them
- Creating scenarios to test your partner's love or commitment
- Purposely engaging in arguments to see how you handle conflict

1. Avoidance:

- Avoiding romantic movies or songs out of fear they'll trigger doubts
- Steering clear of attractive people to prevent questioning your commitment
- Avoiding deep conversations with your partner for fear of finding incompatibilities

1. Checking behaviors:

- Repeatedly "checking" your feelings for your partner
- Monitoring your physical reactions when around your partner (e.g., do you get butterflies?)
- Constantly checking your partner's social media or phone

1. Confessing:

- Feeling compelled to confess every doubt or fleeting attraction to your partner
- Repeatedly apologizing for perceived relationship shortcomings

1. Research and information seeking:

- Excessively reading relationship articles or books
- Constantly searching online for information about "normal" relationships
- Taking numerous online quizzes about love and compatibility

1. Mental rituals:

- Repeating specific phrases in your mind to "neutralize" negative thoughts
- Mentally reviewing all the positive aspects of your relationship
- Counting or other ritualistic mental behaviors when doubts arise

1. Controlling behaviors:

- Trying to control your thoughts or feelings about the relationship
- Attempting to regulate your partner's behavior to alleviate your anxiety
- Excessive planning or organizing to create a "perfect" relationship

As with obsessions, it's the frequency, intensity, and distress associated with these behaviors that distinguish ROCD compulsions from normal relationship behaviors. Individuals with ROCD often recognize that their compulsions are excessive or irrational, but feel unable to stop them.

3.3 Real-Life Examples and Case Studies

To better understand how ROCD manifests in real life, let's look at a few case studies. These examples are composites based on typical presentations of ROCD and do not represent any specific individuals.

Case Study 1: Sarah's Doubt Spiral

Sarah, a 28-year-old marketing executive, has been dating Tom for two years. They have a loving relationship, share similar values, and enjoy spending time together. However, Sarah is plagued by constant doubts about their relationship.

Obsessions:

- "Do I love Tom enough?"
- "What if I'm settling?"
- "Should I be feeling more excited about our future?"

Compulsions:

- Sarah frequently asks Tom if he loves her and if he's happy in the relationship.
- She constantly analyzes her feelings, trying to gauge if she's "in love enough."
- Sarah often compares her relationship to her friends' relationships, searching for signs that her relationship measures up.

Impact: Sarah's ROCD has led to significant anxiety and depression. She finds it difficult to be present in the relationship, always questioning her feelings and decisions. Tom feels confused and hurt by Sarah's constant need for reassurance, creating tension in their otherwise healthy relationship.

Case Study 2: Michael's Perfection Pursuit

Michael, a 35-year-old teacher, has been married to Emma for three years. He loves Emma deeply, but his ROCD manifests as an obsessive focus on her perceived flaws.

Obsessions:

- Fixating on minor physical imperfections in Emma's appearance
- "Is Emma intelligent enough for me?"
- "What if I could find someone more perfect?"

Compulsions:

- Michael frequently compares Emma to other women, both physically and intellectually.
- He researches extensively about relationships, seeking confirmation that it's normal to notice partner's flaws.
- Michael creates mental checklists of Emma's positive qualities to counteract his negative thoughts.

Impact: Michael's obsession with perfection has created emotional distance in his marriage. He often feels guilty about his thoughts, leading to depression. Emma senses Michael's critical eye and has developed self-esteem issues as a result.

Case Study 3: Lisa's Commitment Conundrum

Lisa, a 31-year-old graphic designer, has been in a relationship with Alex for a year. While she cares for Alex deeply, her ROCD manifests as intense fear of commitment.

Obsessions:

- "What if I'm making a mistake by committing to Alex?"
- "Am I really ready for a long-term relationship?"
- "What if there's someone better out there for me?"

Compulsions:

- Lisa frequently browses dating apps, not to cheat, but to reassure herself that she's not missing out.
- She often creates hypothetical scenarios in her mind, imagining her life with other potential partners.
- Lisa repeatedly asks her friends about their relationships, seeking confirmation that her doubts are normal.

Impact: Lisa's fear of commitment has prevented her from fully investing in her relationship with Alex. She struggles with anxiety and indecisiveness in many areas of her life. Alex feels insecure in the relationship due to Lisa's apparent reluctance to commit.

These case studies illustrate how ROCD can manifest in different ways, but with common themes of doubt, anxiety, and compulsive behaviors. In each case, the individual's ROCD symptoms significantly impact both their own well-being and the health of their relationship.

It's crucial to remember that ROCD is a mental health condition, not a reflection of the relationship's actual quality or the individual's true feelings. With proper diagnosis and treatment, individuals with ROCD can learn to manage their symptoms and enjoy healthy, fulfilling relationships.

In the next chapter, we'll explore the underlying causes of ROCD, which will help us understand why these obsessions and compulsions develop and persist.

The Root Causes of ROCD

Understanding the root causes of Relationship Obsessive-Compulsive Disorder (ROCD) is crucial for both those experiencing it and the professionals treating it. Like many mental health conditions, ROCD doesn't have a single, clear-cut cause. Instead, it's believed to result from a complex interplay of biological, psychological, and environmental factors. In this chapter, we'll explore these different factors and how they contribute to the development of ROCD.

4.1 Biological Factors

Biological factors play a significant role in the development of OCD, including its relationship-focused subtype, ROCD. These factors are largely related to brain structure, function, and chemistry.

Genetic Predisposition

Research suggests that there's a genetic component to OCD:

- Family studies have shown that OCD is more common among first-degree relatives of those with OCD than in the general population.
- Twin studies indicate that genetic factors account for 45-65% of the variance in OCD symptoms.

While no single "OCD gene" has been identified, multiple genes are likely involved, each contributing a small effect to OCD susceptibility.

Brain Structure and Function

Neuroimaging studies have revealed differences in brain structure and function in individuals with OCD:

- The orbitofrontal cortex, anterior cingulate cortex, and striatum are often overactive in individuals with OCD. These areas are involved in decision-making, emotion regulation, and habit formation.
- There may be reduced connectivity between regions responsible for cognitive control and those involved in fear and habit formation.

These structural and functional differences may contribute to the persistent, intrusive thoughts and repetitive behaviors characteristic of OCD and ROCD.

Neurotransmitter Imbalances

Neurotransmitters, the chemical messengers in the brain, also play a role in OCD:

- Serotonin: Many effective OCD treatments involve increasing serotonin levels, suggesting that serotonin dysregulation may contribute to OCD symptoms.
- Dopamine: This neurotransmitter, involved in reward and motivation, may also play a role, particularly in the compulsive aspects of OCD.
- Glutamate: Recent research suggests that abnormalities in glutamate neurotransmission may contribute to OCD symptoms.

These neurotransmitter imbalances may contribute to the anxiety, intrusive thoughts, and compulsive behaviors seen in ROCD.

Hormonal Factors

Hormones may also play a role in OCD and ROCD:

- Some individuals experience onset or exacerbation of OCD symptoms during times of hormonal change, such as puberty, pregnancy, or menopause.
- Fluctuations in sex hormones like estrogen and testosterone may influence OCD symptoms, which could be particularly relevant for ROCD given its focus on romantic relationships.

While these biological factors create a predisposition to OCD and ROCD, they don't determine whether an individual will develop the disorder. Environmental and psychological factors also play crucial roles.

4.2 Psychological Factors

Psychological factors interact with biological predispositions to influence the development and maintenance of ROCD. These factors often relate to an individual's thought patterns, beliefs, and cognitive processes.

Cognitive Distortions

Individuals with ROCD often exhibit certain cognitive distortions or thinking errors:

- All-or-nothing thinking: Viewing the relationship in black and white terms, e.g., "If I have any doubts, it must mean I don't truly love my partner."
- Catastrophizing: Assuming the worst possible outcome, e.g., "If I make the wrong choice about this relationship, my life will be ruined."
- Overestimation of threat: Perceiving normal relationship challenges as dire threats to the relationship.

- Intolerance of uncertainty: Struggling to accept the inherent uncertainties in relationships.

These distortions can fuel the obsessive thoughts characteristic of ROCD.

Attachment Styles

Attachment theory suggests that early relationships with caregivers shape our expectations and behaviors in adult relationships:

- Insecure attachment styles, particularly anxious attachment, may predispose individuals to ROCD.
- Those with anxious attachment often fear abandonment and may be hypervigilant about their relationships, aligning with ROCD symptoms.

Perfectionism

Many individuals with ROCD exhibit perfectionist tendencies:

- They may have unrealistic expectations of what a "perfect" relationship should look like.
- The need for certainty and "getting it right" in relationships can fuel ROCD doubts and compulsions.

Low Self-Esteem

Low self-esteem can contribute to ROCD in several ways:

- It may lead to doubts about deserving love or a good relationship.
- It can fuel fears of abandonment or rejection.
- It might cause individuals to fixate on perceived flaws in themselves or their partners.

Metacognitive Beliefs

Metacognitive beliefs - beliefs about one's own thoughts - can play a role in ROCD:

- Overimportance of thoughts: Believing that having a thought about relationship doubt means the doubt must be true or important.
- Need for control over thoughts: The belief that one should be able to control all thoughts about the relationship.

These beliefs can increase the distress associated with intrusive thoughts and drive compulsive behaviors.

Learned Behaviors

From a behavioral perspective, ROCD can be seen as a learned response:

- Compulsions provide temporary relief from anxiety, reinforcing the behavior through negative reinforcement.
- Over time, this cycle becomes ingrained, making it difficult to break without intervention.

Understanding these psychological factors is crucial for effective treatment, as many therapeutic approaches for ROCD focus on addressing these underlying cognitive and behavioral patterns.

4.3 Environmental and Social Influences

While biological and psychological factors create a predisposition to ROCD, environmental and social influences often play a crucial role in its development and maintenance.

Family Dynamics

Family experiences can significantly impact how individuals approach relationships:

- Growing up in a household with high conflict or divorce may lead to relationship anxiety.
- Parents who model excessive reassurance-seeking or relationship doubt may inadvertently teach these behaviors.
- Family emphasis on perfectionism or high achievement may contribute to unrealistic relationship expectations.

Cultural and Societal Pressures

Societal norms and cultural expectations about relationships can influence ROCD:

- Media portrayals of "perfect" relationships may set unrealistic standards.
- Cultural emphasis on finding "the one" or a soulmate can exacerbate relationship doubts.
- Societal pressure to be in a relationship by a certain age may fuel anxiety about relationship choices.

Social Media and Technology

The pervasive nature of social media can exacerbate ROCD symptoms:

- Constant exposure to curated images of "perfect" relationships can fuel comparison and doubt.
- The ability to constantly check on a partner's online activity can enable compulsive monitoring behaviors.
- Dating apps that present seemingly endless options may increase doubts about relationship choices.

Traumatic Experiences

Past traumatic experiences, particularly in relationships, can contribute to ROCD:

- A history of betrayal or infidelity may lead to hypervigilance in future relationships.
- Experiences of sudden loss or abandonment might fuel fears about relationship stability.
- Any form of relationship trauma can create a heightened need for certainty and control in future relationships.

Stress and Life Transitions

Major life stressors or transitions can sometimes trigger or exacerbate ROCD symptoms:

- Significant life changes like moving in together, getting engaged, or having a child can heighten relationship anxiety.
- General life stress (e.g., work stress, health issues) can sometimes manifest as relationship doubts in individuals prone to ROCD.

Educational Experiences

Certain educational experiences may inadvertently contribute to ROCD tendencies:

- An overemphasis on analytical thinking without balancing emotional intelligence may lead some individuals to over-analyze their relationships.
- Lack of comprehensive relationship education may leave individuals ill-equipped to navigate normal relationship challenges.

Peer Influences

Peer relationships and social circles can impact how individuals view their romantic relationships:

- Friends who constantly question their own relationships may normalize excessive doubt.
- Social groups that prioritize "finding the perfect match" may inadvertently fuel relationship anxiety.

Previous Relationship Experiences

Past romantic experiences naturally shape how individuals approach future relationships:

- A series of unsuccessful relationships may lead to heightened anxiety about making the "right" choice.
- Positive past relationships might be idealized, creating unrealistic standards for current relationships.

Understanding these environmental and social influences is crucial because they often provide the context in which ROCD develops and is maintained. Moreover, addressing these factors can be an important part of treatment and recovery.

It's important to note that while we've discussed biological, psychological, and environmental factors separately, in reality, these factors interact in complex ways. For example, a biological predisposition to anxiety might interact with perfectionistic tendencies and societal pressures to create the conditions for ROCD to develop.

Moreover, the factors that contribute to the development of ROCD may be different from those that maintain it. For instance, while genetic factors may create a predisposition, learned behaviors and cognitive patterns often play a larger role in maintaining the disorder.

Understanding these root causes of ROCD is not just academically interesting - it has important implications for treatment. Effective treatment often involves addressing multiple contributing factors:

- Medication might be used to address biological factors like neurotransmitter imbalances.
- Cognitive-behavioral therapy can help individuals identify and change problematic thought patterns and behaviors.
- Mindfulness-based approaches can help individuals relate differently to their thoughts and feelings.
- Relationship education and couples therapy might address some of the social and environmental factors contributing to ROCD.

By understanding the complex interplay of factors that contribute to ROCD, individuals and their loved ones can approach the disorder with greater compassion and insight. This understanding also underscores the importance of seeking professional help, as effective treatment often requires addressing multiple aspects of the disorder.

Remember, having risk factors for ROCD doesn't mean an individual will definitely develop the disorder, and not having risk factors doesn't mean they won't. ROCD, like all mental health conditions, is complex and multifaceted. If you recognize symptoms of ROCD in yourself or a loved one, it's important to seek help from a mental health professional who can provide a proper diagnosis and treatment plan.

The Cycle of ROCD: How It Perpetuates Itself

Relationship Obsessive-Compulsive Disorder (ROCD) operates in a cyclical pattern that, once established, can be difficult to break without intervention. Understanding this cycle is crucial for both individuals experiencing ROCD and their loved ones, as it provides insight into why the condition persists and how it can be addressed. In this chapter, we'll explore each stage of the ROCD cycle in detail.

5.1 Trigger Events

The ROCD cycle typically begins with a trigger event. These triggers can be external situations or internal experiences that set off relationship-related obsessions. It's important to note that triggers aren't inherently problematic; it's the individual's interpretation and response to these triggers that fuel the ROCD cycle.

Common ROCD triggers include:

1. Partner behaviors:

- Your partner forgetting an important date
- Your partner showing affection differently than usual
- Your partner expressing interest in a hobby you don't share

1. Comparative situations:

- Seeing a seemingly "perfect" couple on social media
- Hearing about a friend's romantic gesture
- Watching a romantic movie or TV show

1. Relationship milestones:

- Moving in together
- Getting engaged
- Celebrating an anniversary

1. Personal stressors:

- Work-related stress
- Health concerns
- Financial worries

1. Internal cues:

- Noticing a fleeting attraction to someone else
- Realizing you haven't thought about your partner all day
- Experiencing a moment of irritation with your partner

1. Uncertainty-provoking events:

- A minor disagreement with your partner
- Your partner expressing doubts or insecurities
- Making future plans together

1. Physical or emotional states:

- Feeling tired or irritable

- Experiencing a low mood
- Hormonal changes

It's crucial to understand that these triggers don't cause ROCD; rather, they activate pre-existing tendencies in individuals prone to ROCD. The way one interprets and responds to these triggers determines whether they'll lead to the next stage of the ROCD cycle.

5.2 Intrusive Thoughts and Doubts

Following a trigger event, individuals with ROCD experience intrusive thoughts and doubts about their relationship. These thoughts are typically unwanted, distressing, and feel difficult to control. They often contradict the individual's true feelings and values, which is part of what makes them so upsetting.

Common intrusive thoughts in ROCD include:

- "What if I don't really love my partner?"
- "Is this relationship right for me?"
- "Am I attracted enough to my partner?"
- "What if I'm making a huge mistake by staying in this relationship?"
- "Does my partner really love me?"
- "Are we compatible enough?"

These thoughts often take the form of "what if" questions or worst-case scenarios. They may fixate on specific aspects of the relationship or partner, or they may be more general doubts about the relationship as a whole.

Key characteristics of ROCD intrusive thoughts:

1. Persistence: These thoughts tend to repeat over and over, feeling impossible to dismiss.
2. Intrusiveness: They pop into the mind unbidden, often at inopportune moments.

3. Ego-dystonic nature: The thoughts often go against the individual's true feelings and values, which is part of what makes them so distressing.
4. Doubt-centric: They typically revolve around uncertainty and doubt, questioning aspects of the relationship that the individual may have previously felt sure about.
5. Catastrophic thinking: They often jump to worst-case scenarios or extreme conclusions.

It's important to note that having occasional doubts or questions about a relationship is normal and can even be healthy. What sets ROCD thoughts apart is their persistent, intrusive nature and the significant distress they cause.

5.3 Anxiety and Distress

The intrusive thoughts and doubts characteristic of ROCD inevitably lead to feelings of anxiety and distress. This emotional response is a crucial part of the ROCD cycle, as it drives the compulsive behaviors that follow.

The anxiety experienced in ROCD can manifest in various ways:

1. Emotional symptoms:

- Feeling of dread or impending doom
- Irritability or mood swings
- Feeling overwhelmed or out of control
- Sense of detachment from oneself or the relationship

1. Physical symptoms:

- Increased heart rate
- Sweating
- Trembling or shaking
- Nausea or stomach discomfort

- Difficulty sleeping

1. Cognitive symptoms:

- Difficulty concentrating
- Racing thoughts
- Heightened alertness to relationship "issues"
- Rumination (repetitive negative thinking)

1. Behavioral symptoms:

- Restlessness or agitation
- Avoidance of relationship-related situations or conversations
- Seeking excessive reassurance
- Difficulty making decisions about the relationship

The level of distress experienced can vary from mild unease to severe panic. Often, the anxiety feels disproportionate to the actual situation, which can be confusing and frustrating for both the individual with ROCD and their partner.

This anxiety serves several functions in the ROCD cycle:

1. It reinforces the perceived importance of the intrusive thoughts. The intense emotional reaction makes the thoughts feel more significant and "true."
2. It creates a strong urge to do something to alleviate the discomfort, setting the stage for compulsive behaviors.
3. It can interfere with logical thinking and problem-solving, making it difficult to challenge the ROCD thoughts rationally.
4. Over time, it can lead to a conditioned fear response to relationship-related triggers, perpetuating the cycle.

Understanding the role of anxiety in ROCD is crucial for breaking the cycle.

Many therapeutic approaches for ROCD involve learning to tolerate this anxiety without resorting to compulsive behaviors.

5.4 Compulsive Behaviors and Temporary Relief

In an attempt to alleviate the anxiety and distress caused by intrusive thoughts, individuals with ROCD engage in compulsive behaviors. These behaviors are intended to reduce anxiety, gain certainty, or prevent feared outcomes. While they may provide temporary relief, they ultimately reinforce the ROCD cycle.
Common compulsive behaviors in ROCD include:

1. Reassurance seeking:

- Repeatedly asking your partner if they love you
- Constantly checking in with friends about the state of your relationship
- Excessively researching relationship advice online

1. Checking and testing:

- Mentally reviewing past interactions for signs of problems
- Creating scenarios to test your or your partner's feelings
- Constantly monitoring your emotional state around your partner

1. Comparing:

- Excessively comparing your relationship to others
- Comparing your current relationship to past relationships or idealized notions of love

1. Confessing:

- Sharing every doubt or negative thought with your partner
- Confessing attractions to others, even when insignificant

1. Avoidance:

- Avoiding situations that might trigger relationship doubts
- Putting off making future plans due to uncertainty
- Emotionally distancing yourself from your partner

1. Overanalyzing:

- Excessively analyzing every aspect of your relationship
- Overthinking casual remarks or interactions

1. Rituals:

- Engaging in superstitious behaviors related to your relationship
- Repeating certain phrases or actions to "neutralize" negative thoughts

These compulsive behaviors typically provide temporary relief from anxiety. This relief, however, comes at a cost:

1. It reinforces the false belief that the compulsive behavior is necessary and effective.
2. It prevents the individual from learning that they can tolerate the anxiety without engaging in compulsions.
3. It often creates new problems in the relationship, such as frustrating the partner with constant reassurance-seeking.
4. It takes up significant time and mental energy, interfering with daily life and relationship enjoyment.

Moreover, the relief provided by these compulsions is usually short-lived. The doubts and anxiety typically return, often stronger than before, leading to more intense compulsions. This creates a progressively worsening cycle of obsessions and compulsions.

5.5 Reinforcement of the Cycle

The final stage of the ROCD cycle involves the reinforcement of the entire process, making it more likely to repeat and intensify over time. This reinforcement occurs through several mechanisms:

1. Negative reinforcement: The temporary relief provided by compulsive behaviors negatively reinforces these actions. In other words, the reduction of anxiety (an unpleasant state) strengthens the likelihood of engaging in compulsions in the future.

2. Increased sensitivity to triggers: Over time, individuals with ROCD may become hypersensitive to potential triggers, noticing and reacting to an ever-widening array of relationship-related cues.

3. Cognitive reinforcement: The cycle reinforces belief systems that maintain ROCD, such as the overimportance of certainty in relationships or the belief that all doubts must be resolved.

4. Avoidance learning: As individuals engage in avoidance behaviors to prevent anxiety, they never learn that they can tolerate the discomfort, further reinforcing the avoidance.

5. Relationship strain: The cycle often creates real problems in the relationship (e.g., frustration from constant reassurance-seeking), which then serve as new triggers, perpetuating the cycle.

6. Attentional bias: The cycle trains the individual to be hypervigilant about relationship issues, making them more likely to notice and fixate on potential problems.

7. Emotional conditioning: Over time, relationship-related cues become paired with anxiety through classical conditioning, making it more likely for these cues to trigger the ROCD cycle in the future.

8. Skill deficit: As individuals rely more on ROCD-related coping mechanisms, they may fail to develop healthy relationship skills, making them more reliant on the ROCD cycle.

9. Identity reinforcement: For some, ROCD behaviors may become integrated into their identity (e.g., "I'm just a very careful person in

relationships"), making it harder to recognize and change these patterns.

10. Intermittent reinforcement: Occasionally, the ROCD cycle may lead to genuine relationship improvements (e.g., increased communication), which can intermittently reinforce the cycle, making it particularly resistant to change.

Understanding this reinforcement is crucial for breaking the ROCD cycle. Effective treatment often involves:

- Recognizing the cyclical nature of ROCD
- Learning to tolerate anxiety without engaging in compulsions (exposure and response prevention)
- Challenging the beliefs that maintain the cycle (cognitive restructuring)
- Developing healthier coping mechanisms and relationship skills

Breaking the ROCD cycle is challenging but possible with proper treatment and support. By understanding each stage of the cycle and how it perpetuates itself, individuals with ROCD can begin to interrupt the process and build healthier patterns of thinking and behaving in their relationships.

Remember, if you recognize this cycle in your own life, it's important to seek help from a mental health professional who specializes in OCD. They can provide you with the tools and support needed to break free from the ROCD cycle and build a healthier, more satisfying relationship with both yourself and your partner.

ROCD vs. Genuine Relationship Issues

One of the most challenging aspects of Relationship Obsessive-Compulsive Disorder (ROCD) is distinguishing it from genuine relationship issues. This difficulty can lead to confusion, misdiagnosis, and inappropriate interventions. In this chapter, we'll explore how to differentiate between ROCD and real relationship problems, discuss scenarios where it might be one or the other, and highlight the dangers of misdiagnosis.

6.1 How to Distinguish Between the Two

Distinguishing between ROCD and genuine relationship issues can be complex, as there can be overlap in symptoms and experiences. However, there are several key factors to consider:

1. Nature of the Thoughts ROCD:

- Thoughts are intrusive, unwanted, and ego-dystonic (against one's true feelings and values).
- Doubts tend to be repetitive and cyclical, often without resolution.
- Thoughts focus excessively on "rightness" of the relationship or partner.

1. Genuine Issues:

- Concerns arise from actual experiences or incompatibilities.

- Thoughts are more goal-directed, aimed at problem-solving.
- Focus is on specific, concrete issues in the relationship.

1. Emotional Response ROCD:

- Extreme anxiety, distress, or panic in response to relationship thoughts.
- Feelings of guilt about having doubts.
- Distress feels disproportionate to the actual situation.

1. Genuine Issues:

- Emotional responses, while potentially intense, generally feel proportionate to the situation.
- Less likely to induce panic or extreme guilt about having concerns.

1. Behavioral Patterns ROCD:

- Engaging in compulsive behaviors like excessive reassurance-seeking, checking, or comparing.
- Avoidance of triggers related to relationship doubts.
- Rituals or mental acts aimed at neutralizing thoughts.

1. Genuine Issues:

- Behaviors are more focused on addressing and resolving specific problems.
- May involve seeking advice or support, but not compulsively.
- Less likely to involve ritualistic behaviors.

1. Impact on Daily Life ROCD:

- Significant time spent ruminating about the relationship, interfering with daily activities.

- Distress and compulsions impact work, social life, and other areas of functioning.

1. Genuine Issues:

- While potentially distressing, concerns generally don't dominate thoughts to the same extent.
- Impact on other life areas is usually less severe.

1. History and Pattern ROCD:

- Often a pattern of similar doubts across different relationships or life areas.
- Symptoms may worsen during times of stress or transition.

1. Genuine Issues:

- Concerns are more likely to be specific to the current relationship or situation.
- May not have a history of similar patterns in past relationships.

1. Response to Reassurance ROCD:

- Reassurance provides only temporary relief before doubts return, often stronger.
- Constant need for new forms of reassurance.

1. Genuine Issues:

- Reassurance or addressing concerns often provides lasting relief.
- Less likely to need constant, repetitive reassurance.

1. Content of Concerns ROCD:

- Often focuses on abstract concepts like "rightness" or "true love."
- May fixate on minor flaws or issues that objectively don't threaten the relationship.

1. Genuine Issues:

- Concerns usually relate to concrete, significant aspects of the relationship.
- Focus on issues that objectively could impact relationship satisfaction or compatibility.

Understanding these differences can help individuals, partners, and professionals better identify whether ROCD or genuine relationship issues are at play. However, it's important to note that these categories aren't always mutually exclusive – it's possible for someone with ROCD to also have genuine relationship concerns.

6.2 When It's ROCD and When It's Not

To further clarify the distinction between ROCD and genuine relationship issues, let's explore some scenarios:

Scenario 1: Constant Doubts About Love

ROCD: Sarah constantly questions whether she truly loves her partner, despite feeling happy in the relationship. These thoughts are intrusive and distressing, contradicting her desire to be in the relationship. She repeatedly asks her partner and friends for reassurance, but the relief is short-lived.

Not ROCD: Michael has been feeling disconnected from his partner for months. He's not sure if he's still in love, based on a gradual change in his feelings and a growing sense of incompatibility. While distressing, these thoughts don't feel intrusive or panic-inducing.

Scenario 2: Concerns About Partner's Attributes

ROCD: Tom is happily married but becomes intensely anxious when he notices his wife's minor flaws, like the sound of her laugh. He spends hours analyzing whether these "flaws" mean they're incompatible, despite otherwise being satisfied with the relationship.

Not ROCD: Emily is concerned about her boyfriend's anger issues, which have led to hurtful arguments. She's contemplating whether this is a deal-breaker for their relationship, based on concrete experiences and values.

Scenario 3: Comparison to Other Relationships

ROCD: Lisa constantly compares her relationship to those of her friends and social media acquaintances. She feels intense anxiety that her relationship might not measure up, leading her to repeatedly seek validation from her partner and obsessively monitor other couples' interactions.

Not ROCD: David notices that his friends' relationships seem more affectionate than his own. This observation leads him to have a constructive conversation with his partner about increasing intimacy and quality time together.

Scenario 4: Concerns About Attraction

ROCD: James is in a loving relationship but becomes extremely distressed when he finds other people attractive. He constantly "checks" his attraction to his partner and others, feeling guilty and anxious about what these feelings might mean.

Not ROCD: Olivia has noticed a gradual decline in her attraction to her partner over the past year, coinciding with a decrease in emotional intimacy. She's considering whether this is a sign that they've grown apart.

Scenario 5: Worries About the Future

ROCD: Megan experiences intense anxiety about whether her relationship will last forever. Despite being happy with her partner, she constantly seeks reassurance about the future and becomes distressed by any uncertainty.

Not ROCD: Alex is unsure about his long-term compatibility with his partner due to differing views on marriage and children. He's contemplating these issues thoughtfully, without excessive anxiety or compulsive behaviors.

These scenarios illustrate that while both ROCD and genuine relationship issues can involve doubts and concerns, the nature of these thoughts, the emotional response, and the resulting behaviors often differ significantly.

6.3 The Danger of Misdiagnosis

Misdiagnosing ROCD as simply relationship problems, or vice versa, can have serious consequences. Here are some of the dangers associated with misdiagnosis:

1. Inappropriate Interventions Misdiagnosing ROCD as relationship issues:

- May lead to unnecessary relationship counseling that doesn't address the underlying OCD.
- Could result in premature relationship termination if ROCD is mistaken for incompatibility.
- Might reinforce ROCD patterns if the focus is on resolving specific doubts rather than addressing the OCD cycle.

1. Misdiagnosing relationship issues as ROCD:

- Could lead to ignoring real relationship problems that need addressing.
- Might result in unnecessary medication or OCD-specific therapies.
- May prevent couples from developing necessary relationship skills or addressing incompatibilities.

1. Worsening of Symptoms For ROCD:

- Misdiagnosis can lead to continued engagement in compulsions, worsening the OCD cycle.
- Focusing on relationship content rather than OCD processes can increase doubt and anxiety.
- Lack of proper treatment can lead to chronic, worsening symptoms over time.

1. For relationship issues:

- Treating genuine problems as ROCD might lead to suppression of valid concerns.
- Could result in staying in an unfulfilling or unhealthy relationship.

1. Impact on Self-Esteem and Mental Health

- Misdiagnosis in either direction can lead to feelings of confusion, self-doubt, and frustration.
- For those with ROCD, lack of proper diagnosis can reinforce beliefs about being "too picky" or "not cut out for relationships."
- For those with genuine relationship issues, misdiagnosis as ROCD might lead to doubting their own judgment and perceptions.

1. Strain on the Relationship

- Misdiagnosis can create additional stress and confusion for both partners.
- May lead to inappropriate coping strategies that strain the relationship further.
- Could result in loss of trust if one partner feels their concerns are being dismissed or pathologized.

1. Delayed Proper Treatment

- Misdiagnosis means that the real issue – whether ROCD or relationship problems – goes unaddressed.
- This delay can lead to entrenched patterns that are harder to treat over time.
- For ROCD, delayed treatment can result in the disorder expanding to other life areas.

1. Financial and Time Costs

- Pursuing the wrong type of intervention can be costly in terms of both money and time.
- This can lead to disillusionment with the therapeutic process, potentially discouraging future help-seeking.

1. Missed Opportunities for Growth

- Misdiagnosis of ROCD might prevent individuals from learning valuable OCD management skills.
- Misdiagnosing relationship issues as ROCD could prevent couples from developing important relationship skills and insights.

To avoid these dangers, it's crucial to seek assessment from mental health professionals who are knowledgeable about both OCD and relationship dynamics. A thorough evaluation should consider:

- The individual's history, including past relationships and mental health
- The nature and pattern of the thoughts and doubts
- The presence of compulsive behaviors
- The impact on daily functioning and the relationship
- The couple's dynamic and communication patterns

In some cases, a period of observation or trial interventions may be necessary to clarify the diagnosis. It's also important to remember that ROCD and relationship issues can coexist, and both may need to be addressed for optimal well-being.

Ultimately, whether the issue is ROCD, genuine relationship concerns, or a combination of both, the goal is to foster healthier, more satisfying relationships and improved individual well-being. By accurately distinguishing between these issues, individuals and couples can receive the most appropriate and effective support and interventions.

The Impact of ROCD on Relationships

Relationship Obsessive-Compulsive Disorder (ROCD) can have profound and far-reaching effects on both the individual experiencing it and their romantic partners. These impacts can extend to other relationships as well, including family and friends. In this chapter, we'll explore the multifaceted ways in which ROCD affects relationships, from the immediate emotional toll to the potential long-term consequences if left untreated.

7.1 Effects on the Individual with ROCD

ROCD can significantly impact the individual experiencing it in various ways:

1. Emotional Distress:

- Persistent anxiety and worry about the relationship
- Feelings of guilt and shame about having doubts
- Mood swings related to obsessive thoughts
- Depression stemming from constant relationship uncertainty

1. Cognitive Impacts:

- Difficulty concentrating on tasks unrelated to the relationship
- Constant mental preoccupation with relationship doubts

- Indecisiveness about relationship matters
- Distorted perceptions of the relationship and partner

1. Behavioral Changes:

- Engaging in time-consuming compulsions (e.g., seeking reassurance, checking)
- Avoidance of triggers related to relationship doubts
- Procrastination on making relationship decisions or commitments
- Decreased engagement in previously enjoyed activities

1. Self-Esteem and Identity:

- Lowered self-esteem due to persistent doubts and perceived inadequacies
- Confusion about one's own feelings and desires
- Difficulty in forming a stable sense of self within the relationship
- Self-doubt about one's capacity for love or maintaining relationships

1. Physical Health:

- Sleep disturbances due to racing thoughts or anxiety
- Appetite changes related to stress
- Physical symptoms of anxiety (e.g., stomach upset, muscle tension)

1. Social Impacts:

- Withdrawal from social situations to avoid relationship triggers or comparisons
- Difficulty in maintaining friendships due to preoccupation with ROCD
- Reluctance to discuss relationship issues with others for fear of judgment

1. Work or Academic Performance:

- Decreased productivity due to preoccupation with relationship thoughts
- Difficulty meeting deadlines or maintaining focus
- Increased absenteeism due to ROCD-related stress

1. Relationship Satisfaction:

- Decreased ability to enjoy positive aspects of the relationship
- Constant feeling of relationship dissatisfaction, even in objectively good relationships
- Difficulty in emotional and physical intimacy due to doubts

1. Decision-Making:

- Paralysis in making relationship-related decisions
- Difficulty committing to long-term plans with a partner
- Second-guessing past relationship decisions

1. Coping Mechanisms:

- Reliance on unhealthy coping strategies (e.g., excessive reassurance-seeking)
- Difficulty in developing healthy relationship skills due to ROCD preoccupations

These effects can create a significant burden for the individual with ROCD, impacting nearly every aspect of their life. The constant doubts and anxiety can be exhausting, leading to a decreased quality of life and overall well-being.

7.2 Effects on Partners and Loved Ones

ROCD doesn't just affect the individual experiencing it; it can also have substantial impacts on their romantic partners and other loved ones:

1. Emotional Impact on Partners:

- Feelings of confusion and hurt due to perceived lack of commitment
- Frustration with constant reassurance-seeking
- Anxiety about the stability of the relationship
- Feelings of inadequacy or unlovability due to partner's doubts
- Emotional exhaustion from managing partner's ROCD symptoms

1. Communication Challenges:

- Difficulty in having conversations unrelated to ROCD concerns
- Reluctance to share personal thoughts or feelings for fear of triggering doubts
- Misunderstandings due to ROCD-influenced interpretations of interactions
- Breakdown in effective communication patterns over time

1. Relationship Dynamics:

- Imbalance in emotional labor within the relationship
- Development of codependent patterns (e.g., partner becoming primary source of reassurance)
- Loss of spontaneity and fun due to ROCD preoccupations
- Decreased intimacy (both emotional and physical)

1. Trust Issues:

- Erosion of trust due to constant questioning of the relationship
- Partner's loss of confidence in the stability of the relationship
- Difficulty in making future plans together

1. Behavioral Adaptations:

- Partner modifying their behavior to avoid triggering ROCD symptoms
- Reluctance to express needs or concerns to avoid adding to ROCD stress
- Taking on more responsibilities to compensate for ROCD-related difficulties

1. Impact on Shared Social Life:

- Withdrawal from social activities as a couple
- Strain on relationships with family and mutual friends
- Difficulty in maintaining a united front in social situations

1. Personal Growth and Independence:

- Partner may put personal goals or growth on hold to manage relationship concerns
- Loss of independence as partner becomes enmeshed in ROCD cycles

1. Mental Health of Partners:

- Increased risk of anxiety or depression in partners
- Development of caregiver fatigue or burnout
- Possible emergence of their own relationship doubts or insecurities

1. Financial Impact:

- Potential financial strain due to ROCD-related issues (e.g., missed work, therapy costs)
- Difficulty in making joint financial decisions or commitments

1. Effects on Children (if applicable):

- Exposure to relationship tension and uncertainty
- Potential modeling of anxious relationship behaviors

- Inconsistency in parenting due to ROCD preoccupations

It's important to note that while these effects can be significant, many partners of individuals with ROCD show remarkable patience, understanding, and resilience. With proper education about ROCD and support, partners can play a crucial role in the recovery process while also maintaining their own well-being.

7.3 Long-Term Consequences if Left Untreated

If ROCD is left untreated, it can lead to several long-term consequences that can significantly impact both the individual with ROCD and their relationships:

1. Chronic Relationship Dissatisfaction:

- Persistent feelings of doubt and uncertainty in relationships
- Inability to fully enjoy or appreciate positive aspects of relationships
- Decreased overall life satisfaction due to constant relationship stress

1. Relationship Instability:

- Increased likelihood of relationship breakdown or divorce
- Pattern of short-term relationships due to inability to commit
- Difficulty in forming new relationships due to entrenched ROCD patterns

1. Worsening of ROCD Symptoms:

- Expansion of ROCD concerns to other areas of life (e.g., career decisions, friendships)
- Increased severity and frequency of obsessions and compulsions over time

- Development of additional mental health issues (e.g., depression, generalized anxiety)

1. Social Isolation:

- Withdrawal from social relationships due to ROCD-related anxiety
- Loss of support network over time
- Difficulty in maintaining friendships or family relationships

1. Career Impact:

- Potential for career stagnation due to difficulty in making decisions or commitments
- Decreased job performance or job loss due to ROCD-related stress and preoccupation
- Missed opportunities for advancement or personal growth

1. Self-Esteem and Identity Issues:

- Chronic low self-esteem due to persistent self-doubt
- Difficulty in forming a stable sense of self independent of relationship status
- Internalized beliefs about being "flawed" or "incapable of love"

1. Physical Health Consequences:

- Chronic stress leading to various health issues (e.g., cardiovascular problems, weakened immune system)
- Potential for stress-related disorders (e.g., IBS, chronic pain)
- Neglect of physical health due to mental preoccupation

1. Financial Consequences:

- Potential financial instability due to relationship breakdowns or job issues
- Costs associated with untreated mental health issues over time
- Missed financial opportunities due to difficulty in making commitments

1. Impact on Future Generations:

- If parenting while struggling with untreated ROCD, potential for passing on anxious attachment styles or OCD tendencies to children
- Strain on family relationships over time

1. Missed Life Experiences:

- Reluctance to engage in new experiences or take risks due to relationship anxiety
- Regret over missed opportunities for love and connection
- Limited personal growth and self-discovery

1. Increased Vulnerability to Other Mental Health Issues:

- Higher risk of developing other anxiety disorders or depression
- Potential for substance abuse as a coping mechanism
- Increased risk of suicidal thoughts in severe, untreated cases

1. Relationship Skill Deficits:

- Failure to develop healthy relationship skills due to ROCD preoccupations
- Difficulty in emotional regulation within relationships
- Challenges in effective communication and conflict resolution

1. Trust Issues:

- Development of pervasive trust issues that extend beyond romantic relationships
- Difficulty in forming close bonds with others due to fear of uncertainty

1. Cognitive Patterns:

- Entrenchment of negative thought patterns and cognitive distortions
- Difficulty in rational decision-making, especially regarding relationships

It's crucial to emphasize that these long-term consequences are not inevitable. With proper treatment and support, individuals with ROCD can learn to manage their symptoms effectively, leading to healthier, more satisfying relationships and improved overall quality of life. Early intervention is key to preventing these long-term impacts and promoting recovery.

Treatment for ROCD typically involves a combination of cognitive-behavioral therapy (CBT), particularly exposure and response prevention (ERP), and sometimes medication. Many individuals with ROCD find significant relief from their symptoms with appropriate treatment, allowing them to build and maintain healthy, fulfilling relationships.

If you recognize ROCD patterns in yourself or a loved one, seeking professional help is an important step towards preventing these long-term consequences and working towards recovery. Remember, ROCD is a treatable condition, and with the right support, it's possible to break free from the cycle of doubt and anxiety and build the loving, stable relationships you desire.

Self-Assessment: Do I Have ROCD?

If you've been experiencing persistent doubts and anxiety about your relationship, you may be wondering whether you're dealing with Relationship Obsessive-Compulsive Disorder (ROCD). While a definitive diagnosis can only be made by a mental health professional, self-assessment tools can help you gain insight into your symptoms and determine whether seeking professional help might be beneficial. In this chapter, we'll explore some self-assessment methods, how to interpret your results, and guidance on when to seek professional help.

8.1 Questionnaires and Checklists

Self-assessment questionnaires and checklists can be valuable tools for identifying potential ROCD symptoms. Here are two types of assessments you can use:

ROCD Symptom Checklist

Consider how often you experience the following thoughts or behaviors in your relationship:

1. I constantly question whether I truly love my partner.
2. I obsessively compare my relationship to others' relationships.
3. I frequently doubt if my partner is "the one" for me.
4. I spend excessive time analyzing minor flaws in my partner's appearance

or personality.

5. I feel intense anxiety when I'm uncertain about aspects of my relationship.
6. I constantly seek reassurance from my partner or others about my relationship.
7. I have intrusive thoughts about potentially being happier with someone else.
8. I feel compelled to "check" my feelings for my partner regularly.
9. I worry excessively that I might be making a mistake by staying in this relationship.
10. I spend a lot of time researching relationship advice or taking online compatibility tests.
11. I avoid making future plans with my partner due to relationship uncertainty.
12. I frequently confess every doubt or negative thought to my partner.
13. I struggle to enjoy positive moments in my relationship due to persistent doubts.
14. I often question if I'm attracted enough to my partner.
15. I feel the need to mentally review past interactions with my partner to check for problems.

Rate each item on a scale of 0 to 4: 0 - Never 1 - Rarely 2 - Sometimes 3 - Often 4 - Very Often

Relationship-Centered and Partner-Focused ROCD Scales

For a more comprehensive assessment, consider these two scales that focus on different aspects of ROCD:

Relationship-Centered ROCD Scale:

1. I constantly assess how "right" this relationship feels.
2. I can't stop thinking about whether I really love my partner.
3. I check and recheck my feelings towards my partner.

4. I constantly try to figure out how I feel about my relationship.
5. I continually doubt my feelings for my partner.
6. I'm constantly looking for evidence that this is the "right" relationship.

Partner-Focused ROCD Scale:

1. I constantly think about my partner's flaws.
2. I can't stop comparing my partner's qualities to those of others.
3. I question whether my partner is "right" for me.
4. I obsess over whether I could be happier with someone else.
5. I worry that my partner isn't intelligent enough.
6. I'm preoccupied with doubts about my partner's attractiveness.

Rate each item on a scale of 0 to 4: 0 - Never 1 - Rarely 2 - Sometimes 3 - Often 4 - Very Often

Additional Questions

To provide more context for your responses, consider these additional questions:

1. How much time per day do you spend thinking about these relationship concerns?
2. To what extent do these thoughts and behaviors interfere with your daily life and activities?
3. How much distress do these thoughts and behaviors cause you?
4. Have you noticed these patterns in previous relationships?
5. Do you engage in any repetitive behaviors to alleviate your relationship anxiety?

8.2 Interpreting Your Results

After completing these self-assessment tools, it's important to interpret your results thoughtfully. Here's how to approach your scores:

ROCD Symptom Checklist

Add up your scores for all 15 items:

- 0-15: Low likelihood of ROCD. Your relationship concerns are likely within the normal range.
- 16-30: Moderate likelihood of ROCD. You may be experiencing some ROCD symptoms.
- 31-45: High likelihood of ROCD. Your symptoms suggest a strong possibility of ROCD.
- 46-60: Very high likelihood of ROCD. Your symptoms strongly indicate ROCD, and professional help is recommended.

Relationship-Centered and Partner-Focused ROCD Scales

For each scale, add up your scores for the 6 items:

- 0-6: Low likelihood of this type of ROCD.
- 7-12: Moderate likelihood of this type of ROCD.
- 13-18: High likelihood of this type of ROCD.
- 19-24: Very high likelihood of this type of ROCD.

Interpreting Your Overall Results

When interpreting your results, consider the following:

1. Severity of Symptoms: Higher scores generally indicate more severe symptoms. However, even moderate scores can be significant if they

cause substantial distress or interfere with your daily life.

2. Pattern of Symptoms: Look for patterns in your responses. Do you score higher on relationship-centered or partner-focused items? This can give insight into the nature of your ROCD symptoms.

3. Frequency and Intensity: Pay attention to how often you experience these thoughts and how intense they are. Frequent, intense symptoms are more indicative of ROCD.

4. Impact on Daily Life: Consider how much these thoughts and behaviors affect your daily functioning, relationships, and overall well-being.

5. Duration of Symptoms: ROCD symptoms typically persist over time. If you've been experiencing these symptoms for several months or more, it's more likely to be ROCD.

6. Distress Level: ROCD symptoms cause significant distress. If your relationship thoughts and behaviors are causing you considerable anxiety or interfering with your ability to enjoy your relationship, this is a strong indicator of ROCD.

7. Ego-Dystonic Nature: ROCD thoughts often feel alien or against your true feelings and values. If you find your thoughts distressing and inconsistent with what you believe you truly feel, this aligns with ROCD.

Remember, these self-assessment tools are not diagnostic instruments. They are meant to help you recognize patterns and determine whether further evaluation might be beneficial. A high score doesn't necessarily mean you have ROCD, and a low score doesn't guarantee you don't. These tools are just one part of understanding your relationship thoughts and behaviors.

8.3 When to Seek Professional Help

While self-assessment can provide valuable insights, there are several situations in which seeking professional help is advisable:

1. High Scores on Self-Assessments: If you scored in the high or very high ranges on these self-assessment tools, it's a strong indicator that

professional evaluation would be beneficial.

2. Significant Distress: If your relationship thoughts and behaviors are causing you considerable anxiety, sadness, or other emotional distress, professional help can provide relief and coping strategies.

3. Interference with Daily Life: When your relationship concerns are interfering with your work, social life, or ability to engage in daily activities, it's time to seek help.

4. Relationship Strain: If your symptoms are putting a significant strain on your relationship, couples therapy or individual therapy can help address these issues.

5. Compulsive Behaviors: If you find yourself engaging in repetitive behaviors (like constantly seeking reassurance or checking) to alleviate relationship anxiety, professional help can provide strategies to manage these compulsions.

6. Persistent Symptoms: If you've been experiencing these symptoms for several months or more, especially if they've been worsening over time, professional evaluation is recommended.

7. Coexisting Mental Health Concerns: If you're also experiencing symptoms of depression, other forms of anxiety, or any other mental health concerns, a professional can provide comprehensive care.

8. Uncertainty and Confusion: If you're feeling overwhelmed and unsure about what you're experiencing, a mental health professional can help you make sense of your symptoms and provide clarity.

9. Impact on Decision-Making: If ROCD symptoms are preventing you from making important life decisions (like committing to a relationship or moving forward with life plans), professional guidance can be crucial.

10. Desire for Treatment: If you're interested in learning strategies to manage your symptoms and improve your relationship satisfaction, seeking professional help is a positive step.

When seeking professional help, consider the following:

- Look for a mental health professional with experience in OCD, particularly ROCD. Cognitive-Behavioral Therapy (CBT) and Exposure and Response Prevention (ERP) are often effective treatments for ROCD.

- Be prepared to describe your symptoms, their impact on your life, and any patterns you've noticed.
- Remember that seeking help is a sign of strength, not weakness. Many people with ROCD find significant relief with proper treatment.
- If you're in a relationship, consider whether individual therapy, couples therapy, or a combination of both would be most beneficial.
- Be patient with the process. Treatment for ROCD often involves challenging deeply ingrained thought patterns and behaviors, which takes time.

Remember, ROCD is a treatable condition. With proper diagnosis and treatment, many individuals experience significant improvement in their symptoms and overall relationship satisfaction. If you're concerned about your relationship thoughts and behaviors, don't hesitate to reach out to a mental health professional for support and guidance.

Treatment Options for ROCD

Relationship Obsessive-Compulsive Disorder (ROCD) is a challenging condition, but the good news is that several effective treatment options are available. In this chapter, we'll explore the primary treatment approaches for ROCD, including Cognitive-Behavioral Therapy (CBT), Exposure and Response Prevention (ERP), medication options, and mindfulness and acceptance-based approaches.

9.1 Cognitive-Behavioral Therapy (CBT)

Cognitive-Behavioral Therapy (CBT) is one of the most effective and widely used treatments for ROCD. CBT is based on the premise that our thoughts, feelings, and behaviors are interconnected, and by changing our thoughts and behaviors, we can influence our emotions.

Key components of CBT for ROCD include:

1. Cognitive Restructuring:

- Identifying negative thought patterns and cognitive distortions related to relationships
- Challenging these thoughts with evidence and alternative perspectives
- Developing more balanced and realistic thinking about relationships

1. Behavioral Experiments:

- Testing out beliefs about relationships in real-life situations
- Gathering evidence to support or refute relationship-related fears

1. Psychoeducation:

- Learning about ROCD, its symptoms, and how it operates
- Understanding the difference between ROCD thoughts and genuine relationship concerns

1. Skill Building:

- Developing coping strategies for managing anxiety and intrusive thoughts
- Learning healthy relationship skills and communication techniques

1. Relapse Prevention:

- Identifying potential triggers and developing strategies to manage them
- Creating a plan for maintaining progress after therapy ends

The CBT process for ROCD might look something like this:

1. Assessment: The therapist conducts a thorough evaluation of your ROCD symptoms, relationship history, and any co-occurring conditions.
2. Goal Setting: You and your therapist collaboratively set treatment goals, such as reducing the frequency of intrusive thoughts or decreasing reassurance-seeking behaviors.
3. Cognitive Work: You learn to identify and challenge ROCD-related thoughts. For example, if you have the thought "If I have any doubts, it means I don't really love my partner," you might learn to challenge this with "It's normal to have occasional doubts, and they don't negate my overall feelings of love."

4. Behavioral Interventions: You might work on gradually reducing compulsive behaviors, such as excessive reassurance-seeking or checking.
5. Skill Practice: Between sessions, you practice applying CBT techniques to real-life situations and report back on your experiences.
6. Progress Review: You and your therapist regularly review your progress and adjust the treatment plan as needed.

CBT for ROCD typically involves weekly sessions over several months, although the exact duration can vary based on individual needs.

9.2 Exposure and Response Prevention (ERP)

Exposure and Response Prevention (ERP) is a specific type of CBT that is particularly effective for OCD, including ROCD. ERP involves gradually exposing yourself to situations that trigger your ROCD symptoms while refraining from engaging in compulsive behaviors.

The ERP process for ROCD typically involves:

1. Creating an Exposure Hierarchy:

- Listing situations that trigger ROCD symptoms, from least to most anxiety-provoking
- For ROCD, this might include things like "Looking at photos of attractive people" or "Thinking about past relationships"

1. Gradual Exposure:

- Starting with less anxiety-provoking situations and gradually working up to more challenging ones
- Staying in the anxiety-provoking situation until the anxiety naturally decreases

1. Response Prevention:

- Resisting the urge to engage in compulsive behaviors (like seeking reassurance) during and after exposure
- Learning to tolerate uncertainty and anxiety without resorting to compulsions

1. Processing the Experience:

- Discussing the exposure experience with your therapist
- Identifying insights gained and challenges faced

Examples of ERP exercises for ROCD might include:

- Intentionally thinking about relationship doubts without seeking reassurance
- Looking at photos of your partner's ex without comparing yourself
- Watching romantic movies without checking your feelings for your partner
- Deliberately noticing attractive people without engaging in mental rituals

ERP can be challenging, as it involves facing your fears head-on. However, it's one of the most effective treatments for OCD and ROCD. Over time, ERP helps reduce the power of ROCD triggers and builds your ability to tolerate uncertainty in relationships.

9.3 Medication Options

While therapy is often the first-line treatment for ROCD, medication can also play a valuable role, especially in cases where symptoms are severe or when therapy alone isn't providing sufficient relief. The most commonly prescribed medications for ROCD are:

1. Selective Serotonin Reuptake Inhibitors (SSRIs):

- Examples: fluoxetine (Prozac), sertraline (Zoloft), paroxetine (Paxil)
- How they work: SSRIs increase the availability of serotonin in the brain, which can help reduce obsessions and compulsions
- Considerations: It may take several weeks to see the full effects; side effects can include nausea, sleep changes, and sexual dysfunction

1. Serotonin-Norepinephrine Reuptake Inhibitors (SNRIs):

- Examples: venlafaxine (Effexor), duloxetine (Cymbalta)
- How they work: Similar to SSRIs but also affect norepinephrine levels
- Considerations: May be used if SSRIs aren't effective; similar side effect profile to SSRIs

1. Tricyclic Antidepressants:

- Examples: clomipramine (Anafranil)
- How they work: Affect multiple neurotransmitters, including serotonin
- Considerations: Often effective but may have more side effects than SSRIs

1. Antipsychotics (in some cases):

- Examples: risperidone (Risperdal), aripiprazole (Abilify)
- How they work: May be used in low doses as an augmentation to SSRIs in treatment-resistant cases
- Considerations: Used less commonly; require careful monitoring for side effects

Important considerations for medication:

- Medication is typically prescribed by a psychiatrist or your primary care physician.
- It often takes 4-6 weeks to see the full effects of these medications.

- Dosages for OCD/ROCD are often higher than those used for depression.
- Never stop taking these medications abruptly; always consult with your prescribing doctor.
- Medication is often most effective when combined with therapy.

The decision to use medication should be made in consultation with a healthcare professional, considering the severity of your symptoms, your overall health, and your preferences.

9.4 Mindfulness and Acceptance-Based Approaches

In recent years, mindfulness and acceptance-based approaches have gained recognition as valuable tools in treating ROCD. These approaches focus on changing your relationship with your thoughts rather than trying to eliminate them. Two main therapies in this category are:

1. Mindfulness-Based Cognitive Therapy (MBCT): MBCT combines elements of CBT with mindfulness practices. Key components include:

- Mindfulness meditation: Learning to observe thoughts and feelings without judgment
- Decentering: Recognizing thoughts as mental events, not facts
- Staying present: Focusing on the current moment rather than worrying about the future
- Body scan exercises: Increasing awareness of physical sensations

1. Acceptance and Commitment Therapy (ACT): ACT focuses on accepting uncomfortable thoughts and feelings rather than fighting them. Key components include:

- Cognitive defusion: Learning to step back from thoughts and see them as just thoughts, not reality
- Acceptance: Allowing thoughts and feelings to be present without trying

to change them

- Contact with the present moment: Similar to mindfulness, focusing on the here and now
- Values clarification: Identifying what's truly important to you in relationships
- Committed action: Taking steps towards your values, even in the presence of difficult thoughts and feelings

Benefits of mindfulness and acceptance-based approaches for ROCD:

- Reduced reactivity to intrusive thoughts: Learning to observe thoughts without automatically believing or acting on them
- Increased psychological flexibility: Becoming more adaptable in the face of relationship uncertainties
- Improved present-moment awareness: Spending less time ruminating about the past or worrying about the future
- Enhanced self-compassion: Developing a kinder, more understanding attitude towards yourself
- Better emotion regulation: Learning to tolerate difficult emotions without resorting to compulsive behaviors

Practical mindfulness exercises for ROCD might include:

- Mindful observation of relationship doubts without trying to resolve them
- Loving-kindness meditation to cultivate self-compassion and compassion for your partner
- "Leaves on a stream" visualization for letting go of intrusive thoughts
- Mindful engagement in relationship activities, focusing fully on the present experience

These approaches can be particularly helpful for individuals with ROCD who find themselves caught in cycles of overthinking or who struggle with the idea of uncertainty in relationships.

Choosing the Right Treatment Approach

The most effective treatment plan for ROCD often involves a combination of these approaches. For example:

- CBT or ERP as the primary treatment
- Medication to help manage severe symptoms
- Mindfulness practices to supplement therapy and enhance overall well-being

Factors to consider when choosing a treatment approach:

1. Severity of symptoms: More severe symptoms might require a more intensive approach, possibly including medication.
2. Personal preferences: Some people prefer non-medication approaches, while others find medication helpful.
3. Previous treatment experiences: If you've tried one approach before without success, trying a different method might be beneficial.
4. Availability of services: Consider what types of therapy and therapists are available in your area.
5. Comorbid conditions: If you're dealing with other mental health issues alongside ROCD, this may influence the treatment approach.

Remember, treatment for ROCD is not one-size-fits-all. It may take some time to find the right combination of treatments for you. Be patient with the process and maintain open communication with your healthcare providers about what is and isn't working.

With the right treatment approach, many people with ROCD experience significant improvement in their symptoms and are able to build healthier, more satisfying relationships. If you're struggling with ROCD, know that help is available, and recovery is possible.

Self-Help Strategies for Managing ROCD

While professional treatment is often necessary for managing Relationship Obsessive-Compulsive Disorder (ROCD), there are numerous self-help strategies that can complement therapy or provide support between sessions. In this chapter, we'll explore various techniques you can use to challenge intrusive thoughts, reduce compulsive behaviors, practice mindfulness and meditation, and build self-esteem and self-compassion.

10.1 Challenging Intrusive Thoughts

Intrusive thoughts are a hallmark of ROCD. Learning to challenge these thoughts is a crucial skill in managing the disorder. Here are some strategies to help you challenge intrusive thoughts:

1. Recognize the Thought: The first step is to become aware of your intrusive thoughts. Try to catch yourself when you're having an ROCD-related thought. For example, "I'm having the thought that I don't love my partner enough."

2. Label the Thought: Identify the thought as an ROCD thought, not a fact. You might say to yourself, "This is an ROCD thought, not reality."

3. Question the Evidence: Ask yourself:

- What evidence supports this thought?
- What evidence contradicts this thought?

- Am I confusing a thought with a fact?
- Is this thought helpful or productive?

1. Use the Double-Standard Technique: Ask yourself how you would respond if a friend shared this thought with you. Would you agree with them or offer a different perspective?
2. Examine the Worst-Case Scenario: If your intrusive thought were true, what would be the worst that could happen? How likely is this scenario? How would you cope if it did happen?
3. Practice Realistic Thinking: Replace the intrusive thought with a more balanced, realistic thought. For example, instead of "If I have any doubts, I don't really love my partner," try "It's normal to have occasional doubts in a relationship. Overall, I care deeply for my partner."
4. Use the Postponement Technique: When an intrusive thought arises, tell yourself you'll think about it later at a designated time. Often, the urgency of the thought will decrease by that time.
5. Keep a Thought Record: Write down your intrusive thoughts, your emotional response, and a more balanced alternative thought. Over time, this can help you identify patterns and practice reframing.

Remember, the goal isn't to eliminate intrusive thoughts entirely (which isn't possible), but to change your relationship with these thoughts and reduce their impact on your emotions and behaviors.

10.2 Reducing Compulsive Behaviors

Compulsive behaviors in ROCD, such as seeking reassurance or constantly checking your feelings, provide temporary relief but ultimately reinforce the cycle of anxiety. Here are strategies to help reduce these behaviors:

1. Identify Your Compulsions: Make a list of your ROCD-related compulsions. Common ones include asking for reassurance, comparing your relationship to others, or mentally reviewing past interactions.

2. Create a Hierarchy: Rank your compulsions from least to most distressing to resist. This will help you tackle them gradually.

3. Practice Gradual Exposure and Response Prevention: Start with resisting your least distressing compulsion for short periods. Gradually work your way up to more challenging compulsions and longer durations.

4. Delay the Compulsion: When you feel the urge to engage in a compulsion, try to delay it for a set amount of time. Start with short delays and gradually increase the duration.

5. Develop Alternative Responses: Create a list of alternative actions you can take when you feel the urge to engage in a compulsion. This might include deep breathing, physical exercise, or engaging in a hobby.

6. Use Reminder Cues: Place visual reminders around your environment to help you resist compulsions. This could be a rubber band on your wrist or a note on your phone.

7. Practice Mindful Awareness: When you feel the urge to engage in a compulsion, pause and mindfully observe the urge without acting on it. Notice how the urge rises and falls.

8. Celebrate Small Victories: Acknowledge and celebrate each time you successfully resist a compulsion, no matter how small. This positive reinforcement can help motivate continued progress.

9. Seek Support: Share your goals with a trusted friend or partner. They can provide encouragement and help you stay accountable.

Remember, reducing compulsions can initially increase anxiety. This is a normal part of the process. With practice, you'll build tolerance for uncertainty and anxiety will decrease over time.

10.3 Mindfulness and Meditation Techniques

Mindfulness and meditation can be powerful tools for managing ROCD. These practices can help you develop a different relationship with your thoughts and feelings. Here are some techniques to try:

1. Basic Mindfulness Meditation:

- Find a quiet place and sit comfortably.
- Focus your attention on your breath.
- When your mind wanders (which it will), gently bring your attention back to your breath.
- Start with 5 minutes and gradually increase the duration.

1. Body Scan:

- Lie down or sit comfortably.
- Slowly focus your attention on each part of your body, from your toes to the top of your head.
- Notice any sensations without judgment.
- This practice can help ground you when ROCD thoughts are overwhelming.

1. Mindful Observation of Thoughts:

- Imagine your thoughts as leaves floating down a stream.
- As ROCD thoughts arise, visualize placing them on a leaf and watching them float away.
- This helps create distance between you and your thoughts.

1. Loving-Kindness Meditation:

- Focus on generating feelings of kindness and compassion for yourself and your partner.
- Repeat phrases like "May I be happy, may I be peaceful" and "May [partner's name] be happy, may [partner's name] be peaceful."
- This can help counteract negative ROCD thoughts about yourself or your partner.

1. Mindful Engagement in Relationship Activities:

- Choose an activity to do with your partner (e.g., having a conversation, holding hands).
- Fully engage in the present moment, using all your senses.
- When ROCD thoughts arise, gently redirect your attention to the present experience.

1. Three-Minute Breathing Space:

- This quick practice can be done anytime, anywhere:

1. Awareness: Notice your thoughts, feelings, and bodily sensations.
2. Gathering: Bring your attention to your breath.
3. Expanding: Expand your awareness to your whole body and surroundings.
4. Mindful Self-Compassion Break:

- When you're struggling with ROCD thoughts, try this:

1. Acknowledge your suffering: "This is a moment of difficulty."
2. Recognize that suffering is part of being human: "Difficulty is a part of life."
3. Offer yourself kindness: Place your hand on your heart and say, "May I be kind to myself."

Remember, mindfulness is a skill that develops with practice. Be patient with yourself as you learn these techniques.

10.4 Building Self-Esteem and Self-Compassion

ROCD can take a toll on your self-esteem and self-worth. Building self-esteem and practicing self-compassion are crucial for managing ROCD and improving overall well-being. Here are some strategies:

1. Challenge Negative Self-Talk:

- Identify negative self-talk related to your ROCD (e.g., "I'm too needy," "I don't deserve love").
- Challenge these thoughts with evidence to the contrary.
- Replace negative self-talk with more balanced, compassionate statements.

1. Practice Self-Compassion:

- Treat yourself with the same kindness you would offer a good friend.
- When you're struggling, ask yourself, "What would I say to a friend in this situation?"
- Use self-compassionate phrases like "This is difficult, but I'm doing my best."

1. Celebrate Your Strengths:

- Make a list of your positive qualities, skills, and accomplishments.
- Regularly acknowledge your progress in managing ROCD, no matter how small.

1. Set Realistic Goals:

- Break down larger goals into small, achievable steps.
- Celebrate each step you accomplish.

1. Practice Self-Care:

- Prioritize activities that nurture your physical and emotional well-being.
- This might include exercise, healthy eating, adequate sleep, and engaging in hobbies.

1. Develop a Growth Mindset:

- View challenges, including ROCD, as opportunities for growth rather than insurmountable obstacles.
- Use phrases like "I'm learning to manage my ROCD" instead of "I'm bad at relationships."

1. Create a Self-Esteem Journal:

- Each day, write down three things you like about yourself or three things you did well.
- Review this journal regularly, especially when you're struggling with self-doubt.

1. Practice Assertiveness:

- Learn to express your needs and feelings in relationships clearly and respectfully.
- Remember that your needs and feelings are valid and important.

1. Engage in Volunteer Work or Acts of Kindness:

- Helping others can boost your sense of self-worth and put ROCD thoughts in perspective.

1. Use Positive Affirmations:

- Develop a list of positive affirmations that counteract your ROCD-related insecurities.
- Repeat these affirmations daily, especially when ROCD thoughts are strong.

1. Limit Comparison:

- Reduce time spent on social media if it triggers comparison-related ROCD thoughts.
- Remember that you're seeing others' highlight reels, not their full reality.

1. Seek Supportive Relationships:

- Surround yourself with people who uplift and support you.
- Consider joining a support group for individuals with OCD or ROCD.

Remember, building self-esteem and self-compassion is a gradual process. Be patient and gentle with yourself as you practice these strategies.

Implementing Self-Help Strategies

As you work on these self-help strategies, keep the following tips in mind:

1. Start Small: Don't try to implement all these strategies at once. Choose one or two to focus on initially.
2. Be Consistent: Regular practice is key. Try to incorporate these strategies into your daily routine.
3. Be Patient: Progress may be slow and non-linear. This is normal and doesn't mean you're failing.
4. Track Your Progress: Keep a journal to note which strategies are most helpful for you.
5. Combine with Professional Help: These self-help strategies work best when combined with professional treatment.
6. Adjust as Needed: If a particular strategy isn't working for you, it's okay to try a different approach.

7. Practice Self-Compassion: Remember to be kind to yourself throughout this process. Managing ROCD is challenging, and you're doing your best.

By consistently applying these self-help strategies, you can develop a toolbox of techniques to manage your ROCD symptoms effectively. Remember, recovery is a journey, and every small step counts. With time and practice, you can learn to manage your ROCD and build a healthier, more satisfying relationship with both yourself and your partner.

7. Practice Self-Compassion: Remember to be kind to yourself throughout this process. Managing ROCD is challenging, and you're doing your best.

Relationship Strategies for Couples Dealing with ROCD

When one partner in a relationship is dealing with Relationship Obsessive-Compulsive Disorder (ROCD), it can put a strain on both individuals and the relationship as a whole. However, with the right strategies and mutual understanding, couples can navigate these challenges and build a stronger, more resilient relationship. This chapter will explore effective communication techniques, the importance of setting boundaries, ways to support a partner with ROCD, and when and how to seek couples therapy.

11.1 Communication Techniques

Effective communication is crucial for any relationship, but it becomes even more critical when dealing with ROCD. Here are some techniques that can help:

1. Practice Active Listening:

- Give your full attention when your partner is speaking.
- Avoid interrupting or planning your response while they're talking.
- Summarize what you've heard to ensure understanding.

1. Use "I" Statements:

- Express your feelings using "I" statements rather than "You" statements.
- For example, say "I feel anxious when…" instead of "You make me anxious when…"
- This approach reduces defensiveness and promotes understanding.

1. Be Honest and Open:

- Share your thoughts and feelings openly, including those related to ROCD.
- Encourage your partner to do the same.
- Create a safe space where both partners feel comfortable expressing themselves.

1. Avoid Blame and Criticism:

- Focus on the issue at hand rather than attacking your partner's character.
- Instead of "You always seek reassurance," try "I've noticed an increase in reassurance-seeking lately. How can we address this together?"

1. Practice Empathy:

- Try to understand your partner's perspective, even if you don't agree.
- Validate their feelings without necessarily agreeing with their thoughts.
- For example, "I can see how that thought is distressing for you, even though I don't see it the same way."

1. Use Time-Outs:

- If discussions become too heated or overwhelming, agree on a signal to take a break.
- Use this time to calm down and reflect before resuming the conversation.

1. Schedule Regular Check-Ins:

- Set aside time regularly to discuss the relationship and ROCD-related issues.
- This can prevent issues from building up and provide a structured time for difficult conversations.

1. Practice Non-Verbal Communication:

- Be aware of your body language and tone of voice.
- Make eye contact, use a gentle tone, and maintain an open posture to convey openness and care.

1. Use Clarifying Questions:

- If something is unclear, ask for clarification rather than making assumptions.
- For example, "Can you help me understand what you mean by that?"

1. Express Appreciation:

- Regularly express gratitude for your partner's efforts and support.
- Acknowledge progress and small victories in managing ROCD.

Remember, effective communication is a skill that improves with practice. Be patient with yourselves and each other as you work on these techniques.

11.2 Setting Boundaries

Setting healthy boundaries is essential in any relationship, but it becomes particularly important when one partner has ROCD. Boundaries help maintain individual well-being while supporting the relationship. Here's how to set and maintain healthy boundaries:

1. Identify Necessary Boundaries:

- Reflect on what boundaries are needed to maintain your well-being and the health of the relationship.
- Consider boundaries around reassurance-seeking, discussion of ROCD thoughts, and time for individual activities.

1. Communicate Boundaries Clearly:

- Express your boundaries clearly and calmly to your partner.
- Be specific about what is and isn't acceptable.
- For example, "I'm happy to provide reassurance once a day, but more than that becomes overwhelming for me."

1. Respect Each Other's Boundaries:

- Once boundaries are set, make a commitment to respect them.
- Remember that respecting boundaries is an act of love and care for the relationship.

1. Be Consistent:

- Consistently enforce the boundaries you've set.
- Inconsistency can lead to confusion and may reinforce ROCD behaviors.

1. Allow for Flexibility:

- While consistency is important, allow for some flexibility as needs change.
- Regularly review and adjust boundaries as necessary.

1. Set Boundaries Around ROCD Discussions:

- Agree on when and how often to discuss ROCD-related issues.
- This prevents ROCD from dominating all interactions.

1. Maintain Individual Identities:

- Set boundaries that allow each partner to maintain their individual interests and friendships.
- This helps prevent codependency and provides a healthy balance in the relationship.

1. Establish Boundaries with Others:

- Decide together how much to share about ROCD with friends and family.
- Respect each other's privacy while also ensuring necessary support.

1. Create Boundaries Around Seeking Help:

- Agree on expectations regarding professional help and treatment adherence.
- For example, "We agree that attending therapy sessions is a priority for managing ROCD."

1. Practice Self-Care Boundaries:

- Establish boundaries that allow each partner time for self-care activities.
- Recognize that taking care of individual needs benefits the relationship as a whole.

Remember, setting boundaries is not about creating distance, but about fostering a healthy, respectful relationship where both partners' needs are met.

11.3 Supporting Your Partner with ROCD

Supporting a partner with ROCD requires patience, understanding, and a delicate balance between providing help and avoiding enabling ROCD behaviors. Here are some strategies for supporting your partner:

1. Educate Yourself:

- Learn about ROCD to better understand what your partner is experiencing.
- This knowledge can increase empathy and help you respond more effectively.

1. Validate Their Feelings:

- Acknowledge that your partner's distress is real, even if the ROCD thoughts aren't rational.
- Use phrases like "I can see this is really difficult for you" or "It makes sense that you're feeling anxious."

1. Encourage Treatment:

- Support your partner in seeking professional help for ROCD.
- Offer to assist in finding a therapist or accompany them to appointments if they'd like.

1. Avoid Providing Excessive Reassurance:

- While it's natural to want to reassure your partner, excessive reassurance can reinforce ROCD patterns.
- Work with your partner and their therapist to find a balance between support and enabling.

1. Encourage Self-Help Strategies:

- Support your partner in practicing self-help techniques learned in therapy or from reputable sources.
- Offer to practice mindfulness or other coping strategies together.

1. Maintain a Healthy Relationship:

- Don't let ROCD become the sole focus of your relationship.
- Continue to engage in enjoyable activities together and nurture your connection.

1. Practice Patience:

- Recovery from ROCD takes time. Be patient with your partner and the process.
- Celebrate small victories and progress along the way.

1. Take Care of Yourself:

- Remember that you can't pour from an empty cup. Prioritize your own mental health and well-being.
- Seek support for yourself if needed, such as individual therapy or support groups for partners of individuals with OCD.

1. Communicate Your Own Needs:

- While being supportive, it's important to express your own needs and feelings.
- Open, honest communication goes both ways.

1. Avoid Criticism or Blame:

- Refrain from criticizing your partner for their ROCD symptoms.
- Remember that they're not choosing to have these thoughts and behaviors.

1. Create a Calm Environment:

- Try to maintain a calm, stable home environment, as stress can exacerbate ROCD symptoms.
- Work together to reduce overall stress in your lives.

1. Be a Teammate, Not a Therapist:

- While your support is crucial, remember that you're not your partner's therapist.
- Encourage them to rely on professional help for therapeutic interventions.

Supporting a partner with ROCD can be challenging, but your understanding and support can make a significant difference in their recovery journey and the health of your relationship.

11.4 When and How to Seek Couples Therapy

While individual therapy is crucial for the partner with ROCD, couples therapy can also play a valuable role in managing the impact of ROCD on the relationship. Here's guidance on when and how to seek couples therapy:
When to Consider Couples Therapy:

1. Communication Breakdown:

- If you're struggling to communicate effectively about ROCD or other issues.

1. Relationship Dissatisfaction:

• If ROCD is significantly impacting relationship satisfaction for either or both partners.

1. Boundary Issues:

• If you're having difficulty setting or respecting boundaries related to ROCD.

1. Intimacy Problems:

• If ROCD is interfering with emotional or physical intimacy.

1. Caregiver Burnout:

• If the non-ROCD partner is experiencing burnout from supporting their partner.

1. Conflict Resolution Difficulties:

• If you're struggling to resolve conflicts related to ROCD or other issues.

1. Misalignment in ROCD Management:

• If you have different views on how to manage ROCD in the relationship.

1. Major Life Transitions:

• During significant life changes that may exacerbate ROCD (e.g., moving in together, getting married).

1. Desire for Preventive Care:

- Even if things are going well, couples therapy can provide tools to strengthen your relationship.

How to Seek Couples Therapy:

1. Discuss it Together:

- Have an open conversation about the possibility of couples therapy.
- Ensure both partners are on board with the idea.

1. Research Therapists:

- Look for therapists who have experience with OCD/ROCD and couples therapy.
- Consider asking for recommendations from individual therapists or OCD organizations.

1. Check Credentials:

- Ensure the therapist is licensed and has relevant experience and training.

1. Consider Logistics:

- Discuss practical matters like scheduling, location, and cost.
- Some therapists offer teletherapy options, which might be more convenient.

1. Prepare for the First Session:

- Discuss what you both hope to achieve from therapy.
- Be prepared to provide a history of your relationship and the impact of ROCD.

1. Be Open and Honest:

- For therapy to be effective, both partners need to be open and honest during sessions.

1. Commit to the Process:

- Understand that therapy is a process that takes time and effort from both partners.

1. Continue Individual Treatment:

- Couples therapy should complement, not replace, individual therapy for ROCD.

1. Review and Adjust:

- Periodically review whether the therapy is meeting your needs and make adjustments if necessary.

1. Practice Between Sessions:

- Be prepared to work on skills and strategies between therapy sessions.

Remember, seeking couples therapy is a sign of strength and commitment to your relationship. It shows that you're both willing to work on your relationship and face challenges together.

By implementing effective communication techniques, setting healthy boundaries, providing appropriate support, and seeking professional help when needed, couples can navigate the challenges of ROCD together. While ROCD can put strain on a relationship, many couples find that working through these challenges together ultimately strengthens their bond and deepens their understanding of each other.

Living and Thriving with ROCD

While Relationship Obsessive-Compulsive Disorder (ROCD) can present significant challenges, it's important to remember that it's possible not just to live with ROCD, but to thrive despite it. This chapter will explore strategies for accepting uncertainty in relationships, cultivating a healthy relationship with yourself, and building resilience against ROCD flare-ups.

12.1 Accepting Uncertainty in Relationships

One of the core challenges of ROCD is dealing with uncertainty in relationships. Learning to accept uncertainty is a crucial step in managing ROCD and building healthier relationships. Here are strategies to help you embrace uncertainty:

1. Understand the Nature of Uncertainty:

- Recognize that uncertainty is a normal part of all relationships, not just those affected by ROCD.
- Remind yourself that seeking absolute certainty is not only impossible but can be harmful to the relationship.

1. Practice Tolerating Uncertainty:

- Start with small exposures to uncertainty in low-stakes situations.

- Gradually increase your tolerance for uncertainty in your relationship.
- Use mindfulness techniques to sit with the discomfort of uncertainty without reacting.

1. Reframe Your Thoughts About Uncertainty:

- Instead of viewing uncertainty as a threat, try to see it as an opportunity for growth and deepening trust.
- Remind yourself that uncertainty allows for surprise, spontaneity, and excitement in relationships.

1. Use Acceptance Statements:

- Develop and practice using acceptance statements, such as:
- "I accept that I can't be 100% certain about my relationship."
- "Uncertainty is a normal part of love and relationships."
- "I choose to embrace the unknown aspects of my relationship."

1. Focus on the Present:

- When uncertainty about the future triggers ROCD thoughts, bring your attention back to the present moment.
- Practice mindfulness techniques to ground yourself in the here and now.

1. Examine Your Beliefs About Relationships:

- Challenge beliefs that fuel the need for certainty, such as "I must always feel deeply in love" or "The right relationship should never have any doubts."
- Develop more realistic, flexible beliefs about relationships.

1. Embrace the Concept of "Good Enough":

- Recognize that no relationship is perfect, and striving for perfection often leads to dissatisfaction.
- Focus on whether your relationship is "good enough" rather than "perfect."

1. Practice Decision-Making Despite Uncertainty:

- Make small decisions in your relationship without seeking reassurance or over-analyzing.
- Gradually work up to bigger decisions, accepting that you can't predict all outcomes.

1. Learn from Others:

- Talk to couples in long-term relationships about how they deal with uncertainty.
- Read about or attend workshops on embracing uncertainty in relationships.

1. Use Metaphors to Understand Uncertainty:

- Think of your relationship as a journey rather than a destination.
- Visualize holding your relationship lightly, like holding a butterfly, rather than grasping tightly.

Remember, accepting uncertainty doesn't mean you don't care about your relationship. Instead, it means you're choosing to engage fully in your relationship despite not having all the answers.

12.2 Cultivating a Healthy Relationship with Yourself

ROCD often involves a great deal of self-doubt and self-criticism. Cultivating a healthy relationship with yourself is crucial for managing ROCD and building stronger relationships with others. Here are strategies to help you develop a positive relationship with yourself:

1. Practice Self-Compassion:

- Treat yourself with the same kindness and understanding you would offer a good friend.
- Use self-compassionate statements, like "I'm doing the best I can with the resources I have."
- When you're struggling, ask yourself, "What would I say to a friend in this situation?"

1. Develop Self-Awareness:

- Regularly check in with your thoughts, feelings, and bodily sensations.
- Keep a journal to track your emotional patterns and triggers.
- Practice mindfulness to increase your awareness of the present moment.

1. Set Personal Goals:

- Establish goals that are independent of your relationship status.
- Pursue interests and hobbies that bring you joy and fulfillment.
- Celebrate your achievements, no matter how small.

1. Practice Self-Care:

- Prioritize your physical health through regular exercise, healthy eating, and adequate sleep.
- Engage in activities that recharge you emotionally and mentally.

- Learn to say "no" to commitments that drain your energy.

1. Challenge Negative Self-Talk:

- Identify and challenge your inner critic.
- Replace negative self-talk with more balanced, realistic thoughts.
- Use positive affirmations to counter ROCD-related self-doubt.

1. Build a Support Network:

- Cultivate friendships and relationships outside of your romantic partnership.
- Consider joining a support group for individuals with OCD or ROCD.
- Maintain connections with family members who support your growth.

1. Embrace Your Individuality:

- Recognize and celebrate your unique qualities and strengths.
- Avoid comparing yourself to others, especially on social media.
- Remember that your worth is not determined by your relationship status or ROCD symptoms.

1. Practice Forgiveness:

- Learn to forgive yourself for past mistakes or perceived shortcomings.
- Recognize that everyone, including you, is imperfect and deserving of compassion.

1. Invest in Personal Growth:

- Engage in activities that challenge you and promote personal development.
- Read self-help books, attend workshops, or work with a life coach.

- View challenges, including ROCD, as opportunities for growth rather than insurmountable obstacles.

1. Cultivate Mindfulness:

- Practice being present in the moment without judgment.
- Use mindfulness techniques to create space between yourself and your ROCD thoughts.
- Engage in regular meditation or yoga practice to enhance overall well-being.

1. Express Gratitude:

- Keep a gratitude journal, noting things you appreciate about yourself and your life.
- Practice expressing self-gratitude for your efforts in managing ROCD.

1. Set Healthy Boundaries:

- Learn to identify and communicate your personal boundaries.
- Respect your own boundaries as much as you respect others'.
- Recognize that setting boundaries is an act of self-respect and self-care.

Remember, cultivating a healthy relationship with yourself is an ongoing process. Be patient and gentle with yourself as you work on these strategies.

12.3 Building Resilience Against ROCD Flare-Ups

While treatment can significantly reduce ROCD symptoms, it's common to experience occasional flare-ups. Building resilience can help you navigate these challenging periods more effectively. Here are strategies to build resilience against ROCD flare-ups:

1. Develop a Flare-Up Action Plan:

- Create a written plan detailing steps to take when you feel ROCD symptoms intensifying.
- Include coping strategies, support contacts, and reminders of past successes.
- Review and update this plan regularly.

1. Practice Regular Stress Management:

- Engage in stress-reduction activities daily, not just during flare-ups.
- This might include meditation, deep breathing exercises, or progressive muscle relaxation.
- Regular stress management can make you more resilient when ROCD symptoms increase.

1. Maintain Treatment Gains:

- Continue practicing techniques learned in therapy, even when symptoms are less intense.
- Regularly review your ROCD management strategies to keep them fresh in your mind.
- Consider occasional "booster" therapy sessions to reinforce skills.

1. Build a Strong Support System:

- Identify trusted individuals you can reach out to during flare-ups.
- Educate your support system about ROCD and how they can help during difficult times.
- Consider joining an OCD or ROCD support group for ongoing understanding and encouragement.

1. Practice Self-Compassion During Flare-Ups:

- Remind yourself that flare-ups are a normal part of the recovery process, not a failure.
- Use self-compassionate statements like, "This is difficult, but I have the tools to handle it."
- Avoid self-criticism for experiencing a flare-up.

1. Use Cognitive Restructuring:

- Challenge ROCD thoughts using cognitive restructuring techniques learned in therapy.
- Remind yourself that thoughts are not facts and don't necessarily reflect reality.
- Practice replacing ROCD thoughts with more balanced, realistic alternatives.

1. Engage in Healthy Distraction:

- Have a list of engaging activities ready for times when ROCD thoughts are intense.
- These might include hobbies, exercise, or social activities.
- Remember that distraction is a short-term strategy and should be balanced with facing fears.

1. Maintain Routine and Structure:

- Stick to your regular routines as much as possible during flare-ups.
- Structure can provide a sense of normalcy and control during difficult times.

1. Practice Mindfulness and Acceptance:

- Use mindfulness techniques to create distance between yourself and ROCD thoughts.

- Practice accepting the presence of ROCD thoughts without engaging with them.
- Remember the metaphor of thoughts as leaves floating down a stream.

1. Focus on Values-Based Living:

- Remind yourself of your core values and what's truly important to you.
- Make decisions based on these values rather than ROCD fears.
- Engage in activities aligned with your values, even when ROCD symptoms are strong.

1. Use Exposure and Response Prevention (ERP) Techniques:

- Continue to practice ERP exercises, even during flare-ups.
- Gradually expose yourself to ROCD triggers without engaging in compulsions.
- Remember that facing fears can help reduce their power over time.

1. Monitor and Manage Physical Health:

- Pay attention to sleep, nutrition, and exercise, as physical health can impact mental health.
- Be cautious with substances like caffeine or alcohol that might exacerbate anxiety.

1. Practice Gratitude:

- Maintain a gratitude practice, even during flare-ups.
- Focus on aspects of your relationship and life that you appreciate.
- This can help counterbalance the negativity bias often present in ROCD.

1. Learn from Each Flare-Up:

- After a flare-up subsides, reflect on what might have triggered it and how you handled it.
- Use this information to refine your coping strategies and action plan.
- Celebrate the strategies that worked well and the resilience you demonstrated.

1. Communicate with Your Partner:

- If you're in a relationship, communicate openly with your partner about flare-ups.
- Discuss how they can support you while also maintaining healthy boundaries.
- Remember that facing ROCD together can strengthen your relationship.

Building resilience against ROCD flare-ups is an ongoing process. Each time you navigate a flare-up, you're building skills and confidence for future challenges. Remember that seeking help when needed is a sign of strength, not weakness.

By accepting uncertainty in relationships, cultivating a healthy relationship with yourself, and building resilience against flare-ups, you can not only live with ROCD but thrive despite it. Remember that recovery is a journey, and every step forward, no matter how small, is a victory. With persistence, self-compassion, and the right support, you can build a fulfilling life and relationship beyond the constraints of ROCD.

ROCD in Different Types of Relationships

Relationship Obsessive-Compulsive Disorder (ROCD) can manifest in various forms, depending on the type of relationship a person is in. While the core characteristics of ROCD remain consistent—obsessive doubts and compulsive behaviors related to the relationship—its impact can differ significantly based on the relationship's context. This section explores how ROCD affects new relationships, long-term partnerships, LGBTQ+ relationships, and polyamorous relationships, providing insights and strategies for managing ROCD in these diverse scenarios.

13.1 ROCD in New Relationships

New relationships are often filled with excitement, discovery, and the thrill of getting to know someone. However, for individuals with ROCD, this early stage can be a breeding ground for obsessive doubts and fears. The uncertainty inherent in new relationships can trigger ROCD symptoms, making it challenging to enjoy the initial stages of a romantic connection.

The Nature of ROCD in New Relationships

In new relationships, ROCD often manifests as obsessive concerns about the "rightness" of the relationship or the partner. These thoughts might include doubts about whether the person is truly attracted to their partner, whether their partner is "the one," or whether they are settling for someone who is not ideal. These doubts can be exacerbated by the lack of deep familiarity with the partner, as every minor imperfection or difference can be blown out of proportion.

For example, a person with ROCD might fixate on their partner's physical appearance, hobbies, or even trivial habits, questioning whether these qualities are indicative of a mismatch. They may also obsessively compare their current partner to previous partners or an idealized version of a partner, leading to relentless anxiety and second-guessing.

Strategies for Managing ROCD in New Relationships

1. **Acceptance of Uncertainty:** Understanding that no relationship is perfect and that it is normal to have doubts can help reduce the pressure to find certainty in a new relationship. Accepting that it is okay not to have all the answers right away can be a powerful tool in managing ROCD.

2. **Focusing on the Present:** Encouraging mindfulness and present-moment awareness can help individuals with ROCD enjoy their new relationship without getting lost in hypothetical future scenarios or unrealistic expectations.

3. **Communication:** Openly discussing feelings of doubt with a partner, without letting ROCD dictate the conversation, can build trust and provide reassurance. However, it is essential to ensure that this communication does not turn into constant reassurance-seeking, which can reinforce ROCD symptoms.

13.2 ROCD in Long-Term Partnerships

Long-term partnerships often involve deep emotional bonds, shared experiences, and a commitment to building a life together. However, the stability and routine of a long-term relationship can sometimes trigger ROCD symptoms, particularly as individuals may begin to question the longevity of their relationship or whether they have made the right choice in staying with their partner.

The Nature of ROCD in Long-Term Partnerships

In long-term relationships, ROCD may manifest as obsessive concerns about the relationship's future or the perceived flaws of a partner. These concerns can include thoughts such as, "What if I'm not really in love with my partner?" or "What if I would be happier with someone else?" These doubts can be especially distressing because they challenge the very foundation of the relationship, leading to significant anxiety and emotional turmoil.

Individuals with ROCD in long-term partnerships might also engage in compulsive behaviors, such as excessively analyzing the relationship, seeking reassurance from their partner, or mentally reviewing past interactions to find "evidence" of their true feelings. This constant questioning can erode the sense of security and satisfaction that typically comes with a long-term relationship.

Strategies for Managing ROCD in Long-Term Partnerships

1. **Strengthening the Relationship Foundation:** Engaging in activities that reinforce the emotional connection between partners, such as date nights, shared hobbies, or meaningful conversations, can help mitigate the impact of ROCD by reminding individuals of the positive aspects of their relationship.

2. **Therapeutic Support:** Cognitive-Behavioral Therapy (CBT) and Exposure and Response Prevention (ERP) can be particularly effective in helping individuals with ROCD challenge their obsessive thoughts and reduce compulsive behaviors. Couples therapy can also provide a safe space to address ROCD's impact on the relationship.

3. **Setting Boundaries with ROCD:** Learning to recognize when ROCD is influencing thoughts and behaviors, and setting boundaries around how much mental energy is given to these doubts, can help prevent ROCD from dominating the relationship.

13.3 ROCD in LGBTQ+ Relationships

ROCD can be particularly challenging in LGBTQ+ relationships, where societal pressures, internalized homophobia, or concerns about acceptance can exacerbate obsessive doubts. LGBTQ+ individuals may face unique challenges that influence how ROCD manifests and is experienced.

The Nature of ROCD in LGBTQ+ Relationships

In LGBTQ+ relationships, ROCD may be intertwined with issues related to sexual orientation, gender identity, or societal expectations. For example, an individual might obsess over whether their relationship is "legitimate" in the eyes of others or whether they are truly attracted to their partner given societal norms.

ROCD in LGBTQ+ relationships may also involve doubts about one's sexual orientation or gender identity, leading to obsessive questioning of whether the relationship aligns with one's true self. These doubts can be compounded by the stress of navigating a relationship in a society that may not fully accept or understand LGBTQ+ identities.

Strategies for Managing ROCD in LGBTQ+ Relationships

1. **Affirmation and Self-Compassion:** Affirming one's identity and relationship, and practicing self-compassion in the face of societal pressures, can help reduce the impact of ROCD. Seeking out supportive communities or resources that affirm LGBTQ+ relationships can also provide reassurance.

2. **Challenging Internalized Stigma:** Addressing any internalized homophobia or transphobia that may be contributing to ROCD symptoms can be an important step in managing the disorder. Therapy focused on LGBTQ+ issues can be particularly helpful in this context.

3. **Building a Supportive Network:** Surrounding oneself with supportive friends, family, and community members who affirm the relationship can help counteract the doubts and fears that ROCD may bring. Having a strong support network can also provide a buffer against societal pressures.

13.4 ROCD and Polyamory

Polyamorous relationships, which involve consensual non-monogamy, present a unique context for ROCD. The complexity of managing multiple relationships and the potential for jealousy or insecurity can interact with ROCD in distinct ways.

The Nature of ROCD in Polyamorous Relationships

In polyamorous relationships, ROCD may manifest as obsessive doubts about whether one is truly capable of loving multiple partners or whether one partner is more "right" than another. These doubts can lead to compulsive behaviors such as comparing partners, seeking excessive reassurance from each partner, or constantly analyzing the dynamics of each relationship.

ROCD in polyamory can also involve fears about the sustainability of the relationship structure or concerns about whether one is fulfilling the needs of all partners equally. The added complexity of managing multiple relationships can amplify the anxiety and doubt associated with ROCD.

Strategies for Managing ROCD in Polyamorous Relationships

1. **Clear Communication:** Open and honest communication with all partners about feelings, doubts, and needs is crucial in managing ROCD in polyamorous relationships. Establishing clear boundaries and expectations can help reduce uncertainty and anxiety.

2. **Equality and Fairness:** Ensuring that all partners feel valued and respected can help mitigate the impact of ROCD. This might involve regular check-ins with each partner to discuss the relationship and address any concerns.

3. **Therapy and Support:** Seeking therapy that is affirming of polyamorous relationships can provide valuable tools for managing ROCD. Support groups or communities focused on polyamory can also offer a space to share experiences and gain insights from others in similar situations.

Conclusion

ROCD can present unique challenges depending on the type of relationship, but with the right strategies and support, it is possible to manage these obsessive doubts and maintain healthy, fulfilling relationships. Whether in a new relationship, a long-term partnership, an LGBTQ+ relationship, or a polyamorous relationship, understanding the nature of ROCD and implementing effective coping mechanisms can help individuals and couples navigate this complex disorder and build stronger connections with their partners.

The Role of Technology and Social Media in ROCD

Relationship Obsessive-Compulsive Disorder (ROCD) is a condition that can deeply impact individuals' lives, affecting how they perceive their relationships and causing significant distress through obsessive doubts and compulsive behaviors. In today's digital age, technology and social media have become integral parts of daily life, influencing how people interact with the world and each other. While these tools offer numerous benefits, they can also exacerbate mental health conditions like ROCD. This section explores how social media and technology can intensify ROCD symptoms, provides strategies for managing online triggers, and suggests ways to use technology positively in the recovery process.

14.1 How Social Media Exacerbates ROCD

Social media platforms, such as Instagram, Facebook, and Twitter, are designed to connect people, share experiences, and build communities. However, for individuals with ROCD, these platforms can also become breeding grounds for obsessive thoughts and compulsive behaviors. The nature of social media, which often emphasizes idealized portrayals of relationships and lives, can significantly exacerbate ROCD symptoms.

Comparison and Perfectionism

One of the most significant ways social media exacerbates ROCD is through the constant exposure to curated, idealized versions of other people's relationships. Users often post highlights of their lives, showcasing moments of joy, romance, and connection. For someone with ROCD, these images and posts can trigger obsessive thoughts such as, "Why doesn't my relationship look like that?" or "Am I in the wrong relationship if I don't feel that happy all the time?" This constant comparison can lead to feelings of inadequacy, fueling the belief that their relationship is flawed or less than perfect.

Reassurance-Seeking Behavior

Another way social media can intensify ROCD is by encouraging reassurance-seeking behaviors. Individuals with ROCD might compulsively check their partner's social media profiles, look for signs of their partner's fidelity or interest, or compare their partner's behavior online to that of others. This behavior can create a vicious cycle, where the temporary relief gained from reassurance only reinforces the need to continue these compulsions, worsening the overall symptoms.

Fear of Missing Out (FOMO)

The Fear of Missing Out, commonly known as FOMO, is another social media-driven phenomenon that can exacerbate ROCD. Seeing others engage in seemingly perfect relationships or social activities can trigger doubts about one's own relationship or create anxiety about missing out on a better connection. This can lead to obsessive questioning about the quality of the current relationship, increasing stress and dissatisfaction.

Exposure to Unrealistic Expectations

Social media often perpetuates unrealistic expectations about love and relationships. From viral love stories to influencers showcasing their "perfect" relationships, these portrayals can create an unrealistic standard that individuals with ROCD feel pressured to meet. The constant bombardment of these idealized images can lead to obsessive thoughts about whether their relationship is meeting these standards, driving compulsive behaviors aimed at achieving an unattainable perfection.

14.2 Managing Online Triggers

Given the pervasive nature of technology and social media, it may seem impossible to escape these triggers. However, there are strategies that individuals with ROCD can use to manage their online presence in a way that reduces the impact of these triggers.

Curating a Healthy Online Environment

One effective strategy is to curate a social media feed that minimizes exposure to triggers. This can involve unfollowing accounts that consistently post content that leads to obsessive thoughts or anxiety. Instead, individuals can choose to follow accounts that promote mental well-being, realistic portrayals of relationships, or provide support and resources for ROCD and mental health issues.

Setting Boundaries with Technology

Setting clear boundaries with technology can also help manage ROCD symptoms. This can include limiting the time spent on social media, using apps that monitor and restrict social media usage, or designating specific times of the day for online activities. By creating a structured approach to social media, individuals can reduce the likelihood of falling into obsessive behaviors.

Mindful Social Media Use

Practicing mindfulness while using social media can help individuals become more aware of how certain posts or interactions make them feel. Mindfulness involves paying attention to the present moment without judgment, which can help individuals recognize when they are being triggered by something online. By identifying these triggers in real-time, individuals can take proactive steps to disengage or reframe their thoughts before they escalate into obsession.

Digital Detoxing

Taking regular breaks from social media, often referred to as "digital detoxing," can be beneficial for mental health, particularly for those struggling with ROCD. A digital detox can help reset one's relationship with technology, reduce the compulsion to constantly check social media, and provide space to focus on in-person connections and self-care practices.

Seeking Support Online

While social media can be a source of triggers, it can also offer support. Joining online communities or forums dedicated to ROCD can provide a space to share experiences, seek advice, and connect with others who understand the challenges of living with the disorder. These communities can be a valuable resource for coping strategies and emotional support, making the online experience more positive and less triggering.

14.3 Using Technology Positively in Recovery

Despite its potential to exacerbate ROCD, technology can also be a powerful tool in the recovery process. When used mindfully, technology can support mental health, provide access to resources, and foster connections that aid in managing ROCD symptoms.

Mental Health Apps

There are numerous mental health apps designed to help individuals manage anxiety, stress, and OCD symptoms. Apps that offer guided meditation, cognitive-behavioral therapy (CBT) techniques, or mindfulness exercises can be particularly helpful for individuals with ROCD. These apps can provide daily reminders, track progress, and offer tools that can be used anytime, making them a convenient and accessible option for managing ROCD.

Teletherapy and Online Counseling

The rise of teletherapy has made mental health support more accessible than ever before. Individuals with ROCD can seek therapy from licensed professionals through online platforms, which offer the flexibility of attending sessions from home. Online counseling can be particularly beneficial for those who may not have access to ROCD specialists in their area or who prefer the convenience of remote sessions. Many therapists also offer text-based support or email check-ins, providing ongoing assistance between sessions.

Online Support Groups

In addition to professional therapy, online support groups and forums dedicated to OCD and ROCD can be invaluable resources. These groups allow individuals to connect with others who share similar experiences, providing a sense of community and understanding. Sharing coping strategies, successes, and challenges with others who "get it" can reduce feelings of isolation and offer practical advice for managing ROCD.

Educational Resources and Tools

The internet is a vast repository of educational resources on ROCD and mental health. Individuals can access articles, research studies, and videos that help them better understand their condition and learn about effective treatment methods. Websites run by mental health organizations often provide free tools, such as self-assessment quizzes or downloadable worksheets, that can aid in self-management and recovery.

Journaling and Reflection Tools

Technology can also be used for journaling, which is a therapeutic practice often recommended for individuals with ROCD. Digital journaling apps allow individuals to track their thoughts, emotions, and triggers over time, providing valuable insights into patterns and progress. Journaling can also be used to challenge obsessive thoughts, reflect on therapy sessions, and set goals for recovery.

Positive Reinforcement through Technology

Lastly, technology can be used to reinforce positive behaviors and achievements in the recovery process. Setting up reminders or rewards for completing therapy exercises, practicing mindfulness, or achieving milestones in managing ROCD can provide motivation and encouragement. Apps that offer positive affirmations or daily inspirations can also contribute to a more positive mindset, helping individuals focus on their strengths and progress.

Conclusion

While technology and social media can exacerbate ROCD by fueling obsessive thoughts and compulsive behaviors, they can also play a crucial role in recovery when used mindfully. By curating a healthy online environment, setting boundaries, and using technology to access resources and support, individuals with ROCD can mitigate the negative impact of social media and leverage technology as a powerful tool in their journey towards healing. Balancing the use of technology with mindful practices and real-world connections can help create a more positive and supportive environment for managing ROCD and improving overall mental well-being.

Future Directions in ROCD Research and Treatment

Relationship Obsessive-Compulsive Disorder (ROCD) is a condition that has garnered increasing attention within the psychological and psychiatric communities. As understanding of this disorder deepens, researchers and clinicians are continuously exploring new avenues for treatment and insights into the underlying mechanisms of ROCD. This section delves into emerging therapies, ongoing studies and clinical trials, and the potential breakthroughs on the horizon that could transform how ROCD is understood and managed in the future.

15.1 Emerging Therapies

As the understanding of ROCD evolves, so too does the landscape of treatment options. Traditional approaches, such as Cognitive-Behavioral Therapy (CBT) and Exposure and Response Prevention (ERP), remain the gold standard for treating OCD and its subtypes, including ROCD. However, emerging therapies are beginning to offer new hope for those struggling with this condition. These therapies, which often incorporate advancements in neuroscience, technology, and holistic approaches, are expanding the toolkit available to clinicians and providing patients with more personalized and effective treatment options.

Mindfulness-Based Cognitive Therapy (MBCT)

Mindfulness-Based Cognitive Therapy (MBCT) is an emerging approach that combines traditional cognitive therapy with mindfulness practices. MBCT aims to help individuals with ROCD develop a non-judgmental awareness of their thoughts and feelings, thereby reducing the impact of obsessive doubts and compulsive behaviors. By training patients to observe their thoughts without getting caught up in them, MBCT can help reduce the distress associated with ROCD and prevent the escalation of obsessive cycles.

Early research suggests that MBCT may be particularly effective for individuals with ROCD, as it addresses the tendency to overidentify with intrusive thoughts. By fostering a mindful awareness, patients learn to view their thoughts as transient and not necessarily reflective of reality, which can be a crucial step in breaking the cycle of obsession and compulsion.

Acceptance and Commitment Therapy (ACT)

Acceptance and Commitment Therapy (ACT) is another emerging therapy that has shown promise in treating OCD and its subtypes. ACT focuses on helping individuals accept their thoughts and feelings without trying to change them, while simultaneously committing to actions that align with their values. In the context of ROCD, ACT encourages patients to accept the presence of doubts and uncertainties in their relationship while continuing to engage in meaningful and value-driven behaviors.

One of the key components of ACT is the concept of cognitive defusion, which involves learning to separate oneself from their thoughts. For individuals with ROCD, this can mean recognizing that obsessive thoughts about their relationship do not necessarily have to dictate their emotions or actions. By focusing on their values, such as commitment, love, and connection, patients can reduce the power of ROCD over their lives.

Virtual Reality Therapy (VRT)

Virtual Reality Therapy (VRT) is an innovative and emerging treatment modality that has shown potential in treating various mental health conditions, including OCD. VRT involves the use of virtual environments to simulate real-life scenarios that trigger obsessive thoughts and compulsive behaviors. For individuals with ROCD, VRT can be used to create scenarios that evoke relationship-related doubts, allowing them to confront and manage these thoughts in a controlled and therapeutic setting.

The immersive nature of VRT allows for more intensive and focused exposure therapy, which can be particularly beneficial for those with ROCD. Patients can practice coping strategies and response prevention in a safe environment, helping to reduce the anxiety and distress associated with real-life triggers. As VRT technology continues to advance, it holds the potential to become a powerful tool in the treatment of ROCD.

Neurofeedback

Neurofeedback is an emerging treatment approach that involves training individuals to regulate their brain activity through real-time feedback. In the context of ROCD, neurofeedback can be used to help patients gain greater control over the brain regions associated with obsessive-compulsive symptoms. By learning to modulate their brain activity, individuals can reduce the intensity and frequency of intrusive thoughts and compulsive behaviors.

Although neurofeedback is still in the early stages of research for ROCD, initial studies suggest that it may offer a promising complementary treatment to traditional therapies. As the technology and understanding of brain function continue to evolve, neurofeedback could become a valuable addition to the range of treatment options available for ROCD.

15.2 Ongoing Studies and Clinical Trials

The field of ROCD research is dynamic, with numerous studies and clinical trials currently underway to explore new treatment options and deepen the understanding of this condition. These ongoing efforts are critical for developing evidence-based interventions and improving the quality of care for individuals with ROCD. This section highlights some of the key areas of focus in current ROCD research and the potential implications for future treatment.

Investigating the Efficacy of MBCT and ACT for ROCD

One of the significant areas of ongoing research is the investigation of the efficacy of Mindfulness-Based Cognitive Therapy (MBCT) and Acceptance and Commitment Therapy (ACT) for treating ROCD. These therapies, which have shown promise in other areas of OCD treatment, are now being rigorously tested in clinical trials specifically targeting ROCD.

Researchers are examining how these therapies impact the severity of ROCD symptoms, quality of life, and overall relationship satisfaction. Early results from these studies are encouraging, suggesting that both MBCT and ACT may offer effective alternatives or complements to traditional CBT and ERP. The findings from these trials could pave the way for broader adoption of these therapies in clinical practice.

Exploring the Neural Mechanisms of ROCD

Another critical area of research involves exploring the neural mechanisms underlying ROCD. By using neuroimaging techniques, such as functional magnetic resonance imaging (fMRI) and electroencephalography (EEG), researchers are gaining insights into the brain regions and networks involved in obsessive-compulsive symptoms related to relationships.

Understanding the neural correlates of ROCD can help identify biomarkers that predict treatment response and guide the development of targeted interventions. For example, if certain patterns of brain activity are associated with ROCD, neurofeedback or brain stimulation techniques could be tailored to address these specific patterns, leading to more effective and personalized treatments.

Evaluating the Role of Technology in ROCD Treatment

Given the increasing role of technology in mental health care, several ongoing studies are evaluating the effectiveness of digital interventions for ROCD. These include mobile apps that deliver CBT-based interventions, virtual reality platforms for exposure therapy, and online support communities.

These studies aim to determine how technology can be used to enhance access to care, improve treatment adherence, and provide real-time support for individuals with ROCD. The results of these trials could lead to the development of more accessible and scalable treatment options, particularly for individuals who may not have access to traditional therapy.

Investigating the Impact of Social Media on ROCD

Social media's role in exacerbating ROCD symptoms is another area of active research. Studies are exploring how different aspects of social media use, such as frequency, content, and engagement patterns, influence the severity of ROCD symptoms. Researchers are also examining whether certain types of social media content are more likely to trigger obsessive thoughts and compulsive behaviors.

The findings from these studies could inform the development of interventions that help individuals with ROCD manage their social media use more effectively, reducing the impact of online triggers on their mental health.

Longitudinal Studies on ROCD and Relationship Outcomes

Longitudinal studies are currently being conducted to explore the long-term impact of ROCD on relationship outcomes. These studies follow individuals and couples over extended periods to assess how ROCD influences relationship satisfaction, stability, and overall well-being.

By understanding the long-term effects of ROCD, researchers can identify factors that contribute to positive or negative outcomes and develop interventions that support couples in navigating the challenges of ROCD. These studies are crucial for providing a more comprehensive understanding of the disorder and its implications for relationships.

15.3 Potential Breakthroughs on the Horizon

The future of ROCD research and treatment holds the promise of significant breakthroughs that could revolutionize how this condition is understood and managed. As research progresses and new technologies emerge, several potential breakthroughs are on the horizon that could transform the landscape of ROCD treatment.

Personalized Medicine and Precision Psychiatry

One of the most exciting potential breakthroughs in the treatment of ROCD is the advent of personalized medicine and precision psychiatry. Personalized medicine involves tailoring treatment to an individual's unique genetic, biological, and psychological profile. In the context of ROCD, this could mean developing treatment plans that are specifically designed to address the underlying causes and mechanisms of each person's symptoms.

Precision psychiatry takes this concept further by using advanced technologies, such as neuroimaging and genetic testing, to predict treatment response and optimize therapy. For individuals with ROCD, this could lead to more effective and efficient treatment, reducing the trial-and-error approach that is often necessary in current clinical practice.

Advances in Neurostimulation Techniques

Neurostimulation techniques, such as transcranial magnetic stimulation (TMS) and deep brain stimulation (DBS), are already being used to treat severe cases of OCD. As research continues to refine these techniques, they hold the potential to become more widely used and effective for treating ROCD.

TMS involves using magnetic fields to stimulate specific brain regions associated with obsessive-compulsive symptoms. DBS, on the other hand, involves surgically implanting electrodes that deliver electrical impulses to targeted brain areas. Both techniques have shown promise in reducing OCD symptoms, and ongoing research is exploring their application for ROCD.

As these techniques become more precise and accessible, they could offer a valuable option for individuals with ROCD who do not respond to traditional therapies. Additionally, advances in portable and non-invasive neurostimulation devices could make these treatments more widely available and convenient.

Development of New Pharmacological Treatments

The development of new pharmacological treatments for ROCD is another area with the potential for significant breakthroughs. Current medications for OCD, such as selective serotonin reuptake inhibitors (SSRIs), are not always effective for everyone, and they often come with side effects.

Research into new classes of medications, such as glutamate modulators and serotonin-dopamine activity modulators, is underway. These medications target different neurotransmitter systems in the brain and may offer more effective treatment options with fewer side effects.

Additionally, the exploration of psychedelics, such as psilocybin, for the treatment of OCD is gaining traction. Early studies suggest that psychedelics, when used in a controlled therapeutic setting, may have the potential to reduce obsessive-compulsive symptoms by promoting neuroplasticity and altering brain connectivity.

Integration of Artificial Intelligence (AI) in Treatment

The integration of artificial intelligence (AI) in the treatment of ROCD represents another potential breakthrough on the horizon. AI-driven platforms can analyze vast amounts of data to identify patterns and predict treatment outcomes, enabling more personalized and effective interventions.

AI can also be used to develop digital therapeutic tools that provide real-time feedback and support for individuals with ROCD. For example, AI-powered apps could monitor a user's symptoms, track their progress, and offer tailored therapeutic exercises or coping strategies based on their needs.

As AI technology continues to advance, it could play a significant role in enhancing the delivery and effectiveness of ROCD treatment, making mental health care more accessible and individualized.

Conclusion

The future of ROCD research and treatment is bright, with numerous emerging therapies, ongoing studies, and potential breakthroughs on the horizon. As the understanding of this complex condition deepens, the development of personalized, innovative, and effective treatment options will continue to evolve, offering new hope for individuals struggling with ROCD. Whether through advances in neurostimulation, the integration of AI, or the refinement of psychotherapeutic approaches, the future holds the promise of more comprehensive and tailored care for those affected by this challenging disorder. With continued research and innovation, the goal of alleviating the burden of ROCD and improving the quality of life for individuals and couples affected by this condition is increasingly within reach.

Conclusion: Embracing Love Beyond Doubt

Relationship Obsessive-Compulsive Disorder (ROCD) can be an overwhelming and distressing condition that significantly impacts both individuals and their relationships. However, understanding ROCD, its symptoms, and its treatment options is the first step toward reclaiming one's life from the grips of obsessive doubt. As we conclude this exploration of ROCD, this chapter will recap the key takeaways and offer a message of hope and empowerment to those navigating the complexities of ROCD.

16.1 Recap of Key Takeaways

Throughout this book, we've delved into the intricacies of ROCD, offering insights into its symptoms, causes, and treatment options. Let's revisit some of the most critical points covered.

Understanding ROCD

At its core, ROCD is a subtype of Obsessive-Compulsive Disorder (OCD) that focuses on obsessive doubts and concerns about one's romantic relationship. These doubts often revolve around the "rightness" of the relationship, the partner's suitability, or the individual's own feelings. These obsessive thoughts are accompanied by compulsive behaviors, such as seeking reassurance, constantly analyzing the relationship, or comparing one's partner to others.

ROCD is not the same as normal relationship concerns. The doubts experienced by those with ROCD are intrusive, persistent, and disproportionate, causing significant distress and often leading to avoidance behaviors that can harm the relationship.

Recognizing the Symptoms

One of the first steps in addressing ROCD is recognizing its symptoms. Common obsessions include fears about not loving one's partner enough, doubts about the partner's physical appearance or personality, and concerns about the longevity of the relationship. Compulsions often include seeking reassurance from the partner or others, mentally reviewing interactions, and comparing the relationship to others'.

Understanding these symptoms is crucial for individuals to recognize when they are being influenced by ROCD rather than genuine relationship concerns. Awareness of the symptoms also helps in identifying when professional help may be needed.

Exploring the Causes

The causes of ROCD are multifaceted and can include biological, psychological, and environmental factors. Biological factors may involve genetic predispositions or brain chemistry imbalances, while psychological factors might include low self-esteem, perfectionism, or an anxious attachment style. Environmental influences, such as societal pressures or past relationship experiences, can also play a significant role.

Recognizing these factors is essential for understanding that ROCD is not a personal failing or a sign of an inherently flawed relationship. Rather, it is a complex condition influenced by various factors, many of which are outside the individual's control.

Treatment Options

Effective treatment for ROCD typically involves a combination of therapy, medication, and self-help strategies. Cognitive-Behavioral Therapy (CBT), particularly Exposure and Response Prevention (ERP), is considered the gold standard for treating ROCD. These therapies help individuals confront and manage their obsessive thoughts without resorting to compulsive behaviors.

Emerging therapies, such as Mindfulness-Based Cognitive Therapy

(MBCT) and Acceptance and Commitment Therapy (ACT), offer additional tools for managing ROCD by fostering acceptance of uncertainty and reducing the impact of obsessive thoughts. Medication, such as selective serotonin reuptake inhibitors (SSRIs), may also be prescribed to help manage symptoms.

Self-help strategies, including mindfulness practices, setting boundaries with compulsive behaviors, and building self-compassion, are also crucial in managing ROCD. These strategies empower individuals to take an active role in their recovery and improve their overall well-being.

The Role of Relationships

Throughout the book, we have also emphasized the importance of relationships in the context of ROCD. Whether in new relationships, long-term partnerships, LGBTQ+ relationships, or polyamorous relationships, ROCD can manifest differently but with equally challenging symptoms. Understanding the specific challenges in each type of relationship helps individuals and couples navigate ROCD more effectively.

Communication, mutual support, and setting boundaries are vital components of maintaining a healthy relationship while managing ROCD. Partners can play a significant role in the recovery process by offering understanding, patience, and encouragement.

16.2 A Message of Hope and Empowerment

Living with ROCD can feel like a constant battle against intrusive doubts and compulsive behaviors that threaten to undermine your relationship and your sense of self. However, it is essential to recognize that ROCD is a treatable condition, and with the right support and strategies, you can regain control over your thoughts and feelings.

You Are Not Alone

One of the most critical messages to take away from this book is that you are not alone. ROCD is a condition that affects many people, and you are not the only one struggling with these doubts and fears. Seeking help and connecting with others who understand your experiences can provide comfort and support as you navigate this journey.

Treatment Works

Another vital takeaway is that treatment works. Whether through therapy, medication, or self-help strategies, many individuals with ROCD have found relief and have learned to manage their symptoms effectively. It may take time and persistence, but improvement is possible, and many people go on to lead fulfilling, loving relationships despite their struggles with ROCD.

Acceptance and Self-Compassion

A central theme in managing ROCD is acceptance—accepting that doubts and uncertainties are a part of life and relationships, and they do not have to dictate your happiness or actions. Cultivating self-compassion is equally important. Recognize that ROCD is not a reflection of your worth or your ability to love; it is a condition that requires care and attention, just like any other health issue.

Building a Healthy Relationship with Yourself

While ROCD focuses on doubts about your relationship, it often stems from underlying insecurities or fears about yourself. Building a healthy relationship with yourself—fostering self-love, confidence, and resilience—can significantly impact how you experience and manage ROCD. By strengthening your sense of self, you can reduce the power of ROCD over your thoughts and emotions.

Embracing Uncertainty

One of the most challenging aspects of ROCD is the need for certainty. The quest for absolute certainty in relationships is not only impossible but also counterproductive. Learning to embrace uncertainty, to accept that no relationship is without its challenges or doubts, is a crucial step toward overcoming ROCD. Love, by its nature, involves risk and vulnerability, but it is also a source of deep connection, joy, and growth.

Moving Forward

As you move forward, remember that recovery from ROCD is a journey, not a destination. There will be ups and downs, moments of doubt, and times of clarity. What matters is your commitment to the process, your willingness to seek help, and your dedication to building a life and relationship that align with your values and aspirations.

Whether you are just beginning to recognize the signs of ROCD or have been on this journey for some time, there is hope. With the right tools, support, and mindset, you can overcome the challenges of ROCD and embrace love beyond doubt.

A Future of Love and Growth

In conclusion, ROCD does not have to define your relationships or your life. While it presents significant challenges, it also offers opportunities for growth, self-discovery, and deeper connections. By understanding ROCD, seeking treatment, and embracing a mindset of acceptance and compassion, you can build a future where love is not overshadowed by doubt but is instead a source of strength, joy, and fulfillment.

As you continue on your journey, remember that love is about more than just certainty; it is about trust, connection, and the willingness to grow together through life's uncertainties. Embrace love beyond doubt, and let it be the foundation upon which you build a life rich with meaning, connection, and happiness.